Family Outing

A Guide for Parents of
Gays, Lesbians and Bisexuals

Family Outing

A Guide for Parents of Gays, Lesbians and Bisexuals

Edited by JOY DICKENS

With a Foreword by SIR IAN McKELLEN

PETER OWEN
London & Chester Springs

The editor gratefully acknowledges the Freedom from Religion Foundation for permission to reprint extracts from 'Religious Right', a speech originally presented to the Foundation on 4 December 1992 and first published in *Freethought Today*, Madison, Wisconsin; and *Shakti Khabar*, the magazine for Asian gays, for permission to reprint a letter which first appeared in that publication.

The editor has attempted to obtain all relevant permissions and would like to be notified of any omissions.

PETER OWEN PUBLISHERS
73 Kenway Road London SW5 0RE
Peter Owen books are distributed in the USA by
Dufour Editions Inc. Chester Springs PA 19425–0007

This edition first published in Great Britain 1995

A catalogue record for this book is available
from the British Library

ISBN 0–7206–0961–5

Printed in Great Britain by Biddles of Guildford & King's Lynn.

Foreword

Ever since I came out and was publically honest about my sexuality, my life has changed for the better – no, for the best! One of the greatest new joys is making contact with people whom I should otherwise never have met. That's the nature of the closet. You are closed in and potential friends are closed out.

It was only five years ago that I discovered Parents' Friend. How I wish there had been such people in South Lancashire when I was growing up in the 1950s. There and then, we never spoke about homosexuality: even those of us who had privately begun to realize the nature of our difference from our friends at school, kept mum. At school, at church, at youth clubs and at home there was silence on the subject, with the result that the dispiriting closet closed tightly around me.

These days things can be different, if a young lesbian or gay man lives close to the metropolitan culture of a big city. But for those who are nervous about the gay scene or who live inconveniently far away from it, help is at hand. There are phonelines and befriending groups and a national gay press to keep lonely individuals in touch. The Age of Consent Campaign in 1994 brought wide coverage in the mainstream media, which must have penetrated the sturdiest closet-door. But there is nothing like personal contact, and there, Parents' Friend, if not unique in its attitudes, is particularly effective.

The journey of coming out will be protracted or sudden, depending on one's personality and circumstances. If all goes well, it will begin early with coming out to oneself but end only when there is no one left in the world from whom the truth needs to be withheld. En route to this happy state, the parents will have to be told. I shall always regret that I left it too late to tell my mother and father that their only son was gay. Far too often, talking intimately to the close family is the

5

most nervewracking time for parents as well as for their child.

When I came out to my stepmother, she was 83 and I was 49 – all she said was: 'Thank goodness. I thought you were going to tell me something really awful. I've known you were gay for 30 years or more.' Not everyone is so lucky, as this book amply shows.

The true stories that follow are by turns gripping, upsetting and joyful. Many of them repeat the same pattern. In theatre terms, their plots unfold a potential tragedy and sometimes a melodrama, from which the outcome is often happy comedy. At the point of discovery or coming out, there is emotional confusion. Over and over, there is a catalogue of stress reminiscent of bereavement: 'shock', 'disappointment', 'despair', 'anguish', 'a world turned upside down', 'guilt', 'blame', 'trauma', 'pain', 'utter confusion'. Then, through the worry and the fear, there is improvement day by day and a sense that life can go on. There will be self-education and eventually a new beginning, from which a family can emerge stronger and more enlightened. In the end, 'love continues forever' and settles down into being unconditional.

Throughout these stages, Parents' Friend is standing by to help. I agree with Emily-Rose: 'I would now urge anyone with a gay child to join a group like Parents' Friend.' I should also urge them to read this book and to buy another one to show a friend and another to enlighten a family member, or a teacher or a preacher or a Member of Parliament. There are so many people whose ignorance can badly affect the maturing child. And, in so many hands, this anthology of experience could be invaluable.

Ian McKellen
1994.

Contents

Introduction   9

What is Sexuality?   11

Finding Out   21

Causes   34

Feelings of Bereavement and Loss   41

Seeking Advice   48

Parental Acceptance   52

Parents Coming Out to Others   62

Suicide   71

Groups, Helplines and Contacts   74

PASTELS   83

The Church – Religious Beliefs and Attitudes   89

HIV/AIDS   99

Conclusion   112

Useful Contacts   123

Reading List   126

Introduction

When I announced my intention to produce an anthology of contributions from parents with lesbian, gay or bisexual children, and partners and spouses who have found themselves in love with our gay or bisexual sons or daughters, the pieces began appearing one after another. I was delighted; it has always been difficult to persuade these parents and others to write for our quarterly newsletter.

Parents with lesbian daughters were, as always, reluctant to write, and even with encouragement they remained silent. Lesbians are far less visible than gay men and this seems to be true of parents with lesbian daughters. At Parents' Friend, we have very few members with lesbian daughters, but regular attenders with gay sons and one or two with bisexual sons. Again, we have never had a parent in our group whose daughter has claimed to be bisexual. We have asked heterosexual wives and husbands with lesbian or gay partners to write for us but few women have felt able and no men. We can never balance a book of this nature and we offer no excuses. Such a book depends entirely on its contributors, and its content reflects their particular situations.

Why go to all this trouble to get parents to write and bring it all together to help 'new' parents and others? First, because I know it helps anyone who finds they have non-heterosexual offspring to know they are not alone when they are feeling quite isolated. Secondly, I, like other parents in my situation, would not be able to relate to a man or woman who had not been in this position, but who thought they knew just how I feel now, or felt at the time when my son came out as gay. There is no parent who, on finding they have a lesbian, gay or bisexual son or daughter, feels comfortable with an outsider's views on how to overcome the myriad of emotions around their new status.

When a devastated parent rings the helpline and asks (as has not been uncommon) 'What makes *you* such an expert?', my answer is simply 'Because I've been there, and I know how *I* felt'.

I hope that our sharing our thoughts and feelings with you, the reader, will help you to learn something at least of how it feels to be in our position and how we may choose to deal with it. Whatever your situation, you will surely move on somewhat in your understanding of sexuality and be better able to act as a support when a son or daughter needs a friendly word or simply a hug because of society's tendency to shun or mock those it fears, and its unquestioning belief in the lies and myths surrounding anyone who appears to be different.

I wish to convey my profound gratitude to all those who have contributed. I feel I have shared a journey of discovery with each writer, and I have enjoyed every minute of their company. Each time I have read or typed these pieces – and these have been numerous – I have never failed to be amazed at the impact they have had on me, the mother of a gay son, who had already heard many stories, both good and bad, before asking others to open up honestly to help those still struggling. I hope a similar impression is made on you as you decide how you are going to cope with the sexuality of your child or relative. I can think of few better guides than the words of the Serenity Prayer:

> Grant me the serenity to accept
> things I cannot change, courage to
> change the things I can, and the wisdom
> to know the difference.
>
> *Joy*

Note Some parents chose to use pseudonyms to protect their identities. Others asked me to be sure *not* to change names they feel good about. In any case, I hope readers will understand that being out takes time.

What is Sexuality?

Do not weep. Do not wax indignant. Understand.
Baruch Spinoza

To begin to understand your son's or daughter's sexuality you must first know the meaning of the word used to describe his or her sexual orientation.

What do heterosexuality, homosexuality, lesbianism, bisexuality mean? Where did these words come from? The *Concise Oxford Dictionary* gives the following explanations:

abnormal: exceptional, irregular; deviating from type
bi-:   having two; doubly; in two ways
bisexual: of two sexes; having both sexes in one individual; (of person) sexually attracted by members of both sexes
hetero-:   other, different (frequently opposite to homo-)
heterosexual: (person) characterized by (the normal) attraction to the opposite sex
homo-:   same (frequently opposite to hetero-)
homosexual: (person) who is sexually attracted only by persons of his or her own sex; relating to same sex
lesbian: of homosexuality in women; homosexual woman; (from Lesbos, island in Aegean Sea, home of Sappho)
normal: conforming to standard, regular, usual, typical; free from mental or emotional disorder

These are more acceptable versions of the sort of description I found in old books at the local polytechnic when my

11

son came out to me. From those explanations I was to understand my son to be a deviant or pervert, queer, a sodomite, and I knew that these were lies. My son was no different from any other mother's son and, of course, to me, he was much nicer than many young people.

I found more up-to-date publications which were easier to follow and to believe. They spoke of 'gay' people who were quite ordinary. The words 'normal' and 'abnormal' were not used and I could more easily see homosexuality as natural for those who were attracted to those of the same gender. But I began to ask myself why there had to be categories or labels for our sexual orientation. Why can we not accept each other as we are – unique individuals with much to share?

Society is not only intolerant of difference, but takes delight in verbalizing homophobia. We hear our gay sons being accused of 'wanting to be women', our lesbian daughters of 'hating men', or we are told that 'once they find the right man' they will have no problem in being 'normal'. Bisexuals are 'unable to make up their minds one way or the other'. These derogatory statements were – and still are – heard in many places. The only way for parents to learn to feel able to counter such remarks is to read sensible books on sexuality and to get to know as many non-heterosexuals as possible. Speaking with these people and listening carefully to their experiences will help you to see how hurtful and dishonest such statements really are.

Simply, a homosexual is a person attracted in a caring, loving or sexual way towards another person (or persons) of the same gender. Most homosexual women prefer to call themselves 'lesbian' or 'gay' women. The word 'homosexual' feels too masculine and uncomfortable.

Why is the word 'gay' used to describe homosexuals? It has, in fact, been used since the 1960s. No one knows for sure where it originated but we regularly hear that 'gay' is an odd way of describing 'such sad people'! Not so. Gay people will say they chose this word for themselves, and it's certainly an improvement on the derogatory terms used by the homophobic. What we do not understand we may fear – hence prejudice and discrimination of those who are different in whatever way – size, shape, skin colour, creed, gender and, of course, sexuality.

Many gay people will explain that 'gay' comes from Gay Street, in the heart of New York City's Greenwich village. The bath houses frequented by homosexual men were situated on the corner of Gay Street and Christopher Street. A few blocks down Christopher Street is the site of the old Stonewall Inn, where years of police harassment finally resulted in street fighting and the long overdue gay rebellion against oppression. This was in the summer of 1969 and the area is today regarded as the birth of the Gay Liberation Movement in the USA.

I go along with those who have no idea where the word gay came from, but prefer to see it as shorthand for 'Good As You', which our non-heterosexual children definitely are. Parents who choose this description of a positive state of being will feel surprisingly empowered to accept their child's sexuality.

Nowadays, we may hear some gay men and women use the derogatory term 'queer' to describe themselves. The reclamation of the word deflects its negative usage. Similarly, while the homophobe uses 'dyke' to describe lesbians, the word is now used positively by gay women themselves.

Bisexuals suffer the prejudice shown to gays and also that *from* gays (for reneging on their gayness). Parents, however, can find bisexuality easier, with the chance of marriage to a heterosexual.

I have considered carefully what bisexuality means. This I felt I really had to do, to help me understand my own son. He is bisexual and until he told me I had no idea that there were indeed people like him. If someone asked me to explain my heterosexuality I would not know where to start, so I asked him to explain briefly and decided then to think carefully on what he had said and do my best to understand. This really didn't seem to be sufficient to satisfy my curiosity so I read a bit, thought a lot and came to the following conclusions, which may be correct and may be otherwise, but at least I feel I've done my best. No one has to go along with my views − they are mine and it's for others to look into this for themselves.

I believe, contrary to what many people say, that we are all born with our sexuality intact. Some of us are primarily hetero-

sexual. *There are others then who believe, without doubt, that they are heterosexual – until they begin to have loving and caring feelings for those of the same gender. They may then believe themselves to be homosexual (gay or lesbian) and go along with those feelings quite easily for a shorter or longer time, or maybe forever. Some may later begin to have feelings, again, or at the same time, for those of the opposite gender. Gender in this instance would often be called 'sex' – whichever word we use, it is to do with how we look physically. They are not undecided about their* feelings *– they are certainly not unable to make up their minds, which one might think they could be. They know damned well how they feel. These are real feelings and beautiful. In a free-thinking society, it would be quite in order to go where these deep feelings led. But no. Heterosexuality is seen as the norm and we are expected to adhere rigidly to society's written or unwritten 'laws'. Society's attitude creates the confusion.*

I see sexuality as part of our spiritual self, gender as part of our physical self. Our spirituality is our true self – our physicality is how we are seen *to be and how we are* expected *to act. However, as no one can ever physically touch our spirituality – it is intangible – we cannot physically remove it. It is there forever and can only be tapped into by another person's spirituality – the part of us that holds our emotions. When there is a blending of the spiritual selves, one person's with another's, there in that fusion we find our sexuality. Thought is mind in action, and when our thoughts tell us, through feelings, that we are attracted to this person or that person or a group of people – then, and only then, does the physical (acting on what our mind tells us) choose to act on the emotions engendered – or choose to ignore them. This way it can look as though a person who, up to a certain point in their life believed themself to be heterosexual, sees another side of self, experiencing that emotional blending of spirit with the spirit of someone who may be male, female, heterosexual or not – the latter being of no real consequence. There is that empowering realization of a new dimension. Then comes the choice either to act on their feelings or let them be, this being the one and only uncertainty. To go along with their conditioning or the way of their inner feelings can be the dilemma. Whether to accept their 'other' self or repress/suppress it, will be the question they ask of themselves.*

I am unable to accept the views of those who say we must love or have gentle, caring feelings only for the opposite sex. Life is too short for such inflexible views. We should give and take true love as and when it is presented to us, being guided by our mind, through our emotions – part of our spiritual self – and then our physical self will, even at a very sensitive and impulsive moment, be able to fulfil its needs.

I believe there is no exclusive hetero-, homo-, bisexuality . . . one gentle push either way easily leads to another path of sexuality, each one proving an exciting part of life's experience and not to be missed. As long as we hurt neither ourselves nor anyone else on our journey of discovery, surely what feels right is right.

I hope that those finding themselves with lesbian, gay or bisexual sons or daughters will, at least, attempt to educate themselves a little on what it means to live in a world still learning to understand difference. Hopefully, they will be able to educate others as they learn themselves. The myths have to be banished forever and the truths believed and accepted.

Janice

It has been suggested that most people have the capacity towards bisexuality. I believe that we only need a tiny push one way or the other sexually, and we may feel differently. Either we notice and let it pass or we act upon it. Bisexuality, in itself, does not 'swing' or 'move' – it just is – worthy and valid.

In his 1948 study of human sexual behaviour, Dr Kinsey suggested that human sexuality varies widely from being exclusively heterosexual to exclusively homosexual. Kinsey believed that most people fall somewhere between numbers 0 and 6 on the following scale:

0 *Exclusively heterosexual;*
1 *Predominantly heterosexual, only incidentally homosexual;*
2 *Predominantly heterosexual, but more than incidentally homosexual;*
3 *Equally hetero- and homosexual;*

4 *Predominantly homosexual but more than incidentally hetero-*
   sexual;
5 *Predominantly homosexual, only incidentally heterosexual;*
6 *Exclusively homosexual.*

The Kinsey scale is commonly used as an indicator of percentages of those with hetero-, homo- or bisexual orientation. It has encouraged the use of labels to describe humans and the way we relate to each other sexually. The problem with labels is that they allow for very little individuality or flexibility; their function is to define and categorize.

Bisexuals are subject to prejudice not only from heterosexuals but from some non-heterosexuals also. They may be seen as reneging on their 'gayness', failing to decide whether they are gay or heterosexual, as if bisexuality did not exist. Some gay men and women believe that bisexuals appreciate anti-gay discrimination, so there is no need to mention them when referring to non-heterosexuals, when naming lesbian and gay switchboards, societies or centres. But if I were bisexual and a lesbian or gay society or switchboard excluded mention of bisexuals, I would neither wish to join nor ring for help and support. I would feel uninvited and unwelcome unless the word 'bisexual' was included. Some heterosexuals involved with work around sexuality feel that it is not up to heterosexuals to comment on this or to invite such argument. However, if I draw attention to what I see as a discrepancy and a prejudice against bisexuals, some people may take a fresh look at the issues around oppression and discrimination of a minority. Discrimination is unacceptable whatever its nature.

Whilst on an intensive residential course of HIV/AIDS counselling, I was astounded to hear a tutor in sexual health remark that every time she hears the word 'bisexual' she 'thinks of sex'. I asked why she felt that way. She could not explain. I spent a considerable length of time attempting to help her understand that bisexual people no more spend all their time engaged in sex than do any other sexual beings. Their days and nights are spent in quite ordinary or exceptional ways; their sexuality is that part of their nature stemming from being human, and their orientation is as natural to them as that of heterosexuals or gay women and men.

Her response was: 'Well, I still think of sex when I hear the word "bisexual".' I was left feeling puzzled as to how a tutor in sexual health can learn so little in the course of her work.

To understand a bisexual son or daughter, one has to work through similar feelings to those one has with lesbian or gay offspring – but it can seem more puzzling.

> *One summer's evening, our son, Steve, told his mother and me that he was gay – in fact, bisexual. Our first reaction was one of shock and disbelief. We had always thought that gay people were easily recognizable and like the image portrayed on TV, in some comedy sketches particularly. Steve is not like that at all. He is an outgoing and popular young man with lots of friends of both sexes. Our house was often filled with young people when he lived at home with us and we never questioned that one day he would pair off permanently with one of the lovely young girls who came to our house. Our second reaction was the inevitable fear and analysis of where, as a family, we might have gone wrong.*
>
> *Steve told us that he had been aware of his feelings for many years and, although he had generally kept these feelings to himself, he had confided in a close friend some years ago, who respected the trust placed in him.*
>
> *My wife and I decided that our love for our son was more important than any other feelings we have, such as disappointment that he may never marry and have children of his own. He is, after all, the same person that we have always known. The difference is that we know him better than we did before. He visits often and we feel comfortable with this.*
>
> *In spite of this we felt, privately, that we were now a different sort of family to others and wondered why we were different and why this situation should happen to us.*
>
> *I made contact with Parents' Friend and was invited along to one of their discussion groups. I was surprised to see so many other parents there, encouraged to talk freely about their fears and doubts, and I found that amongst strangers who were in a similar situation, there was no embarrassment. It was such a relief.*
>
> *I learned from the discussions that one in ten people are thought*

to be gay, and, being of a mathematical turn of mind I soon worked out that in Britain, a country with sixty million people, perhaps six million were gay. Add to this twelve million parents of gay people and, say, one brother or sister, and this makes a total of twenty-four million people in families like ours. If you further add grandparents and aunts and uncles, you will see that up to one half the population of this country is in a similar position to ourselves.

So, you see, we are *a normal family. The remainder of the population probably have other difficulties of their own. After all, what is a 'normal family'? Think on these statistics when you are feeling down. It certainly helps me, in trying to come to terms with our situation, to know that we are not alone.*

Matthew

*

Where would I be if I had set views on life and the way it should be lived?

Several years ago my son came out to me as gay. He was still in education and had a wide group of friends, all heterosexual as far as he knew at the time. One day he got drunk and heard himself coming out to all those friends at a party – he felt he had no control over the way the words poured forth – there was no way of stopping them. A hard lesson on over-imbibing!

This is not unusual when a person has become stressed for a length of time and has had to keep something hidden deep down. The next day he spent on the phone attempting to explain all this away due to his drunken state. They all said they hadn't believed him the day before anyway. No one mentioned it again. Only one friend was told it was really the true state of play, and he was fine about it.

At this time my son had a wonderful boyfriend who was much older than himself. Our son was enjoying himself and really getting the best out of both the worlds he inhabited – the gay one and the straight one. It was quite amusing to realize that none of his friends from school had a clue as to who chauffeured him hither and thither. We could always rely on him getting home safely when we weren't around to do this. Our son and his boyfriend had a wonderful relationship.

At the same time, our son began to get very close to one particular female of his own age, although he had lots of friends who were girls and even his teachers were known to remark upon how they flocked round him. Our son couldn't understand all this himself and it took me to explain that he was not putting pressure on the girls at school in any way and they felt comfortable sharing their secrets and problems with him. Their boyfriends began to feel just the opposite and would show their jealousy and make comments about him taking their girlfriends from them, and yet he never showed any wish to meet the girls out of school. Even the boys must have been puzzled about this.

The one friend who knew about our son's gayness suggested that perhaps it might be a good idea for my son to tell the one girl who was getting quite serious that really there was no point in it. He did that after waiting for the whole of the Christmas period to pass, rather than rock the boat at such a family time, when it might most upset his girlfriend. However, when he did tell her, her response was 'Never mind, I still love you and you'll always be my best mate.' This they have remained for many years.

We did worry rather a lot about how hurt she might be when she had such strong feelings for our son, but they both told us the fact that our son was not heterosexual never escaped them but made no difference to the way they felt for each other. They were so young at the time and yet dealt with it all in such an adult way, talking through a lot of issues and sharing their feelings throughout.

Their 'relationship' over the past six months has become more of a friendship and our sons tells me now that he is most definitely bisexual. He has never had any doubt of this and has never 'sat on the fence'. He has always known, but had to work through all the emotions around his sexuality until he was ready to make this statement. He will forever be close to his girlfriend and they will always share their deepest feelings – it has been that kind of deep relationship right from the start.

Does this worry me? It would, if it worried our son. He seems quite happy with the way he is – happy and satisfied to be what-

*ever way he is. He is able to let his life go whichever way it will,
so why should I worry?*

*My real concern is that he is happy and that I know bisexual
people can be very much misunderstood. I feel they have an even
harder time with society (gay or straight) since so many people
think bisexuals are muddled and need to make a decision one
way or the other. They don't. I can only admire the way my son
has so far dealt with his sexuality. I also admire his girlfriend for
the way she has supported him through any bad times they might
have shared – often through other people's attitudes.*

*How do I feel at this point – when our son has neither boy-
nor girlfriend? I suppose just as I did when his lovely boyfriend
crept out of our lives until he felt able to visit us again. But I
know our son is able to meet both his ex-partners in closeness
and friendship. Nothing has changed in this whatsoever.*

*Our bisexual son will always have our love and support. We
treat him as equal to all others and only hope society can see its
way to do the same. This includes both the gay and the straight
society. We wish this too for all bisexual people everywhere and
can only hope our son continues to meet with people who care
about him. Being realistic, we know, after all, he might not, and
we'll still be here for him if the going gets rough, as it does for
each one of us at some time in our lives.*

Phillipa

Finding Out

As a loving mother I felt I knew my son better than anyone else – even his father – and perhaps better than my son himself. I flattered myself! Once he had come out as gay I realized I knew very little of the real person he was. He was only 16 but I never imagined it to be a 'passing phase'. He was always definite and precise about everything, and he did not tell lies. So why should he lie about such an important issue? He was not one for shocking others, rather one for a quiet life.

When our gay friends came to talk with our son at his request, they gleaned the information that he'd known he was different 'for years'. I was *so* sad. I asked him why he hadn't told me before – I was shocked to think he had struggled with all this totally alone, and when he was still so young! He asked me what I could have done.

'Been there for you,' I answered.

'Well you *were*!' was his reply.

I *was* there, yes, but I still find it sad to know that he'd had to deal with it all quite alone – it took unusual strength and courage to 'come out' at such an early age. I'm glad, now, he didn't wait until he was older. It might not have been as easy for him. I have heard countless coming-out stories since that time and some have been horrendous. One gay man rang the helpline and told of his father's reaction to his gayness. He was told to split up with his lover or leave home. He left home. Years later his mother contacted her son to say she didn't think when he left it meant 'for ever'. Parents will make rash statements and demand of their gay children what they would never dare hint at with their heterosexual daughters or sons. If you turned against your child immediately she or he came out, how about getting in touch? Life is too short for procrastination.

Other parents have expressed sadness in finding a child had worked through his or her sexuality alone when s/he knew 'for ever' s/he did not 'fit' amongst his or her friends. These parents were also there for their children but did not, at the time, know just how much their support meant in all other ways. Without this awareness, the telling would perhaps never have happened. Some parents say they would rather not have known, but at least it has given them the chance to learn something new and to deal with prejudices they perhaps did not appreciate they had until confronted by their child's sexuality.

As a parent you may be tempted to ask 'Why me?', 'Why us?' You may feel to blame, and the guilt is overwhelming. You will wonder if you treated your gay son or daughter differently to your other children or the way other families are brought up. Were you too disciplined? He's had girlfriends, she's had a long-term boyfriend. Is she bisexual? Does she really love this woman? Has this older man pushed him into homosexuality? He says he's bisexual but when asked about HIV he said anal sex is not for him. Perhaps he is bisexual or is he gay or just 'mixed up'. In any case, you are mixed up by now.

Gay men and women *do* have close friends of the opposite gender and may have sexual relationships with them. Young people experiment with all manner of things – drugs, cigarettes, alcohol – so why not sex? How else would they know what sex feels like and how different it can be with the right person? The right person may be of the same gender. Children will do what their peers do to conform, but they will be reluctant to say that relationships with the opposite gender leave them unmoved. They instinctively know it is not appropriate, so it is kept secret until they find someone special of the same gender. Even then they will know it is frowned upon and unlikely to be celebrated by siblings, parents, other relations or friends.

Our sons or daughters will at first hear what their friends say about girl- and boyfriends of the opposite gender, try to feel similarly but, deep down, find it impossible. This is where they begin to be the good actors they will have to be for much of their lives. They will be quite shocked when they realize their sexuality is not the same as that of their friends but, until they are old enough to have sexual feelings, their attraction to others of the same gender is nameless. They feel 'different', but why? Their shock is great when it dawns on them – just as it is for parents when they are told by a son or daughter. For years they may struggle, as my own son did, but they get used to the idea. When parents are told, they must start right at the beginning, and this is where your son or daughter will have difficulty in relating to your dismay – they are so relieved to tell you that it is *you* who take on the burden.

When there is some doubt in your child's mind as to her or his true sexuality it can be difficult to sit back and wait for your son or daughter to decide on the correct definition. Being used to decision-making, you, the parent, may rebel, wanting to know for sure. Some will never label themselves as they see no need for this. It can be dangerous for us to do this for others. It is not for us to assume. At Parents' Friend we often have parents who ring the line, having guessed their child is not heterosexual and wanting it confirmed. We cannot do this, and if their son or daughter is not ready, they have to sit it out – be patient. Only in their own time can each child tell.

When you find 'by accident' that your child is not heterosexual, often that letter has been left purposely for you to see, or that magazine has been 'hidden' in a place you will most certainly come across it. You may be anxious to deny the fact of your child's sexuality or be so angry that you will confront them. When a word as strong as 'confront' is used by callers, it points to the denial, distress and devastation a parent is feeling. Whenever and however you discover it, you must try to calm down enough for rational discussion with your daughter or son. *It is essential to carry on talking.*

The next stage is to find others who have already had this experience and can help and support you. This is when parents' helplines can be useful. You should be offered information and literature to aid your understanding. You must educate yourself in order to accept your gay or bisexual daughter or son. Parents' Friend has a regularly updated booklist, available by post when you send an s.a.e. The more lesbian, gay or bisexual people you can talk with the better – it can be an enormous help. Get to know your son's or daughter's friends to see how they are as people. There are pleasant gay people, angry lesbians, loving bisexuals, angry gay men, happy lesbians and fun-loving bisexuals, just as there are heterosexuals with different personalities. Getting to know your children's friends is useful regardless of their sexuality.

When I first found my son to be gay, I spent weeks telling myself he didn't look gay, until I took myself in hand and accepted there was no 'look' that was gay – I was, in fact, trying to see something that wasn't there. I expected him to have changed, but this was impossible. He was not different now – he always *was* gay.

Parents who ring the helpline will ask if, when 'the phase' is over, their child can 'change back' to how they were before. We have to explain that when someone says they are lesbian, gay or bisexual, that's exactly what they are and always were. They were born that way, so, they cannot 'change back'. I could not become a lesbian, since I was born heterosexual. I could choose lesbian behaviour, but since I know how society frowns on lesbian or gay people this would be unlikely, just as it is unlikely that your child was inveigled into being lesbian, gay or bisexual.

When you are tempted to ask your child how s/he knows s/he is right about his or her gayness or bisexuality, first ask yourself when you realized your sexuality. You will say you always knew, won't you? No one forced you to be heterosexual, so why think your daughter was forced, or chose, to be lesbian? Heterosexuals know they are heterosexual and don't even think about it. It's natural. When we bring our children up to be heterosexual, we do not usually think to let them know that there are some people who are not like us. This is why our lesbian, gay or bisexual offspring have to go through the process of realizing non-heterosexuals exist. They pick up the vibes that non-heterosexuals are unacceptable to society, and especially in the family. In fact, 'those people' do not seem to have families at all. When our children accept that *they* are lesbian, gay or bisexual, and thus 'unacceptable', it takes a long time for them to know that it is OK to be who they are and to wish to tell others. That's when parents receive the shock.

Is it not odd that, upon learning of their daughter's or son's sexuality, parents may instantly wonder what they do in bed – in spite of knowing they've never had the opportunity to be in bed with anyone? Those hearing that a man is gay will routinely relate this to anal sex when, in fact, many gay men say they are as repulsed by this idea as they are to think of a male-female sex act. What they say they need is love, affection, closeness, hugs, kisses, caresses – just as heterosexuals do. After all, heterosexual couples indulge in anal sex in spite of its illegality. Many heterosexuals would find this repulsive.

If you worry about HIV/AIDS (especially if you have a gay son), do you worry about your heterosexual children to the same degree? If not, why not? Everyone is responsible for having safer sex, even parents. It is not who you sleep with, after all, but what you do and how safely. It is not only gay men who contract the HIV virus, or indeed any other sexually transmitted disease. Whatever our sexuality it behoves us to take care when in a sexual relationship or on a one-night stand.

On receiving the news of your child's sexuality you will not perceive, at that moment, the whole new world about to open up to you. There is a vast number of opportunities to learn, and they cost little in monetary terms. If you have a desire to understand and are determined to reach the ultimate goal of total acceptance, the mystery tour you set out upon will have many rewards, not only for you but for your newly 'out' daughter or son.

No experience in life stands alone and the present is always the mirror of the past, whether we recognize the line or not. Our reactions to offspring are set quite immutably against this backcloth, whether we appreciate it or not, and however unexpected the events that occasion our concern.

Equally, we are all, each and every one of us, separate from those who surround us and, however deep the layers of expectation and conditioning, this fundamental law of humanity applies to our offspring as well. They do not ask to be our daughter or son, they exist purely because of our sexual actions, whether desired as a result or not. Consequently, it is quite irrational and illogical of us to put our viewpoints, opinions and beliefs, either religious or political, or career expectations, upon them. Nevertheless, most parents do fall into that trap and few of us are exceptions to that rule. We are instinctively protective of their welfare and feel deeply worried when we feel that they are at risk. It is against this briefly sketched background that I endeavour, more than two decades afterwards, to recapitulate and recapture the reactions that I experienced when learning that my son was gay.

I had always considered myself to be progressive in attitudes, being a Libertarian Socialist who tried to put into practice sexually free attitudes and teachings with essentially non-religious standards. I was influenced by the works of A. S. Neill and other educationists, and also wished to allow both of my children, a girl and a boy, equal opportunity of expresssion and attitude. My daughter was born in 1948, my son in 1950, and consequently both reached the heady and revolutionary decade of the 1960s as teenagers.

I was suffering the breakdown of my first marriage, brought about by a rapidly growing incompatibility based upon a wide difference of opinion on children's upbringing. The split came to a climax during the revelation that my son was gay. For many then quite irrelevant reasons, I had determined to remain at home until both children had finished A Levels and settled themselves, as was their wish, at teacher training colleges.

My son, Geoff, had obviously taken full advantage of most of the attractive and open attitudes of the 1960s, from its music to its politics and beliefs. By the time of my final departure he had embraced nuclear disarmament, activism for the League Against Cruel Sports, anarchism, High Church ritual and, subsequently, Baptist revivalism on top of an earlier atheism. All in rapid succession, combined with progressive rock music and an intake of soft drugs. He was also surrounded by a wide and colourful group of similar persons and indulged in amusingly varied clothing, including sweeping capes like Batman, plus, of course, shoulder-length hairstyle. His visions of life and activity were kaleidoscopic, but very definite and emphatic, at least for the period that he embraced them. From my point of view he always seemed to have the company of very attractive young females.

What reason had I, therefore, even to suspect that my son, who seemed the very embodiment of the new-found freedoms, was gay?

It took my daughter, who was an equally interesting but very different person, meeting me in a pub, while she was on vacation, to tell me that Geoff was almost certainly gay. She was rightly concerned that I should be aware of this fact, knowing that I would not react in anger, and wished me to consider the implications.

I was staggered by this revelation and at first hardly credited its reality. My next reaction was that it was simply a manifestation of his ability to encompass whatever was exciting and way-out, and consequently was a 'passing phase'. Deeper reflection brought concern and disquiet about his future career as a teacher, since I was aware of the very real discrimination and rejection experienced by a person who is homosexual. It is pertinent to recall that the Act of 1967 (Sexual Offences Act) was hardly dry on the Statute Books and there was a very real reaction in the media against its provisions. Indeed, there were quite inflammatory speeches and articles against gay persons. I did not share this, I am pleased to say, but I was deeply worried.

Meanwhile, back at the training college, Geoff was coming out with the degree of enthusiasm and sincere belief that only he could muster and he joined the Gay Liberation Front. On one never-to-be-forgotten occasion I volunteered myself, plus dilapidated van, to assist removing him from his hall of residence to a bed-sit. After lumbering up and down endless stairs with piles of books and records, I returned to check that all his possessions had been cleared. On opening drawers and cupboards I found he had left notices like 'Glad to be Gay', etc. I hastily collected and destroyed them, fearing the impact on him if they were drawn to the notice of the college. Perhaps a typical 'protective parent' response.

We had already made contact on the issue, and my inference that, as I had already lived through his atheism and anarchism, ritual and baptism, I would probably survive his current phase, received an angry rebuff. After trying to reason with him and asking him to exercise caution, I was frankly told to 'Eff off out of my life'. Although hurt and worried, I had no intention of complying with that request and tried to be supportive despite misgivings. To add to the problem, he acquired a lifestyle that was frankly promiscuous, culminating in a semi-permanent relationship with an individual I considered to be a calculating and

*unprincipled sponger. Had 'he' been a 'she' I would have unhesi-
tatingly classified the person as a hard-hearted gold-digger, purely
mercenary. To make matters worse, we both took an instant dis-
like to each other, which rarely remained unnoticed.*

*However, light dawned on affairs. I fell in love with a woman
who not only accepted Geoff, but was extremely sympathetic to
the entire Lesbian and Gay Movement. As a result of her understanding, I not only lost my worries about my son but became
active in the cause of promoting acceptance and equal opportunities
and rights for lesbians and gays. Because of her special strengths,
I was enabled to come out myself and openly support Geoff.*

*It's been a long journey through the tears – something of a
saga for all concerned – a personal agonizing on my part, engendered
by over-protectiveness and lack of understanding, inflamed and
bedevilled by the fact that we are both very different in our reactions, although similar in our emphatic assertions of belief. Geoff,
in my view, is motivated by emotional response, while I think I
am moved by logical analysis! No doubt he would deny these
comparisons, and he may well be correct in this.*

*But we both are at one on his sexuality and he knows that I
am to be relied upon for public affirmation and support for his
rights and those of others. I have learned a great deal in the process,
perhaps far more than I have given, and as a result have had to
examine all previous preconceptions about sexuality and role-
playing. I am still on this road and am grateful for the learning
process which has led me to the realization that a sexual liberation of gender roles and attitudes must precede or accompany
human liberation from the restrictions and imposed repressions
of conventional society.*

*I now recognize that the greatest method of strait-jacketing and
imprisoning humanity has been the religions – all religions – of
this unhappy world. Their dark doctrines of sin and shame hang
over us and the lives we lead. That religion could display a more
human face can be true – the pity is that, in the main, it has not!*

*It is now apparent that the previously hallowed concept of 'holy
(or unholy?) deadlock' which has strait-jacketed society, is col-
lapsing, and with it goes all the burden of 'till death do us part'
and the misery that this doctrine so often brings to so many ill-
matched couples. Few now believe in the 'no sex before marriage'*

strictures and people experiment in relationships to explore their needs and desires to try to ensure more compatibility with their partners.

What, in any event, makes heterosexual activity so different from lesbian and gay sex? Functionally, it serves the same purpose: sexual release, plus hopefully an expression of human love and compassion, the satisfying of a need for the regard of and desire for partnership with another. If it is simply a satisfaction expressed in a one-night stand, then surely it is no different whether it is lesbian, gay or heterosexual coupling – a simple fact neither to be condemned nor applauded. In fact there are many aspects of sexual activity that are common to all – oral sex and anal sex are two obvious examples of actions undertaken by heterosexuals, lesbians and gays. Why not let us freely admit that we are sexual beings, as part of being human, and the form it takes is a matter of orientation, inclination or choice? It is not a matter for others to control, censure or condemn so long as it only involves mutual consent. It is obviously clearly wrong in the instance of rape. There is a need to teach responsible behaviour and to inculcate ideas of respect for conducting a good relationship and consideration of needs. But we have to free ourselves of all the dark and dismal doctrines of repression, inhibition, condemnation and discrimination that have characterized the dogma of many thousands of years of religious oppression and substitute love, compassion and tolerance.

Parents who go out and educate themselves can do their bit to make the world a more understanding place for their non-heterosexual offspring to live in.

Arthur

The following account provides a counterpoint to Arthur's acceptance and willingness to support his son publicly. The acceptance of a daughter's sexuality is total, but something to be kept from the public domain.

I'd give anything to have my daughter back. She was such a lovely little girl and now she's a stranger, someone we don't know. We never wanted this. We love her just the same and have tried to show this, but – yes – I'm selfish, I just wish there were a pill or injection to make her heterosexual.

Jackie is our youngest daughter and she confided in her sister first, while we were away on holiday, asking her to tell my wife and me when we returned. Betty, my wife, says she felt dead inside and told our GP she'd never be able to accept Jackie's sexuality. We both blamed ourselves and wondered what had gone wrong. We know now that she was born as she is, but in the beginning we felt responsible or that she'd chosen to be lesbian, which we know now, for sure, was not so.

We'd hate our neighbours to find out. It's still a secret after four years. We both feel it would be harder to cope if she lived with us and everyone knew. We feel disappointed and would have wished for better things for her, as you always do for your children.

It was summer when we found out and by Christmas, after attending regular Parents' Friend meetings, where we were able to discuss our concerns about Christmas and how to deal with our daughter's partner when she came to visit for the first time, we were able to welcome Jackie and Sally into our home. Sally was a lovely girl and we got on great, which amazed us. Betty had been dreading this meeting but found it surprisingly easy to put her arms round both of them and hug them. She did admit later when we'd said our goodbyes that, in spite of all that, she couldn't have coped with them together in the same bedroom overnight.

Since then, we've bought ourselves a new bed and moved our old double bed into Jackie's room for the two of them to be together. After all, why split them up when they come to us, when they're sleeping together every night when they're at home? Yes, we've moved on a lot and we've learned from others and been able to give our support to other parents, something we never felt we'd be capable of in the beginning.

I feel that I accepted Jackie's sexuality more easily than Betty but the sense of loss I'm sure was just as great for me as it was for her. It was extremely difficult for us to accept that our daughter was lesbian but it must have been even harder for her to tell us. In being able only to discuss our feelings openly at Parents' Friend meetings, having told no one, we felt and still feel we're keeping a dark secret, and it's a great strain.

I still like to keep the sexual side at the back of my mind and

*don't really think it's any of my business or anyone else's any-
way. I feel, even so, that should they be in the adjacent room
overnight my mind would conjure up all sorts of awful things
and I'd feel just as uncomfortable as Betty. I understand my reaction
is pretty usual for a father finding himself with a lesbian daughter, now I've heard other fathers putting their feelings into words
during Parents' Friend meetings, so this helps me to feel stronger.*

*We find mothers seem, somehow, more able to talk about sexu-
ality in group meetings but Betty still finds it upsetting at times.
What is upsetting for most members, I think, is to hear a step-
parent emphasizing it isn't his or her blood-child who is gay! It's
like stepping out of personal responsibility and saying 'not my
fault'.*

*When your child is gay it makes you look at sexuality in a
way never previously necessary – unless a daughter has become
pregnant, I suppose. It brings about an indescribable stress to a
family. There are so many secrets around it, like 'Grandma wouldn't
understand, she's too old, she'd be too upset. The cousins can't
be told as they're too young, or they have children and they wouldn't
let a gay person near their baby', etc. What I've found over the
years is that it takes us all a different length of time to understand and accept, but if we carry on talking together as a family
– even if the extended family is excluded – then it becomes easier
with time.*

*What we parents have to remember is that our child hasn't
changed, they're still the same person they always were. Life goes
on. Love continues forever. We realized from the beginning that
we'd have to make a concerted effort to educate ourselves – no
one was going to offer us all the answers on a plate. We're glad
we did this and will continue to learn. There's always something
new to understand – life's like that.*

*We can do our bit to help others work through their guilty
feelings. That must mean we've moved on somewhat, but we know
we have a long way to go yet. We are aware it takes time and
never imagined in the beginning we'd be able to get this far. So
that's quite positive, isn't it?*

Edward

The experience of finding you have a non-heterosexual son

or daughter is similar, regardless of your culture or national-
ity. The next letter is from an American father.

*Neither of us came from overly religious backgrounds, but we
did provide our son and daughter with conventional exposure to
religious rituals: baptism, communion, confirmation, Christmas,
Easter and other traditions. Our son was even an altar boy for
four years and I played the organ occasionally in church. For
most of our children's growing-up years we were that archetypical
American family with all those trappings so highly touted by
politicians Pat Robertson and Jerry Falwell. If you know Toys
'R' Us then you'll understand when I say 'Ozzie and Harriet
Were Us'!*

*Our family consists of the requisite father, mother, a son first
and a daughter second. Our children had two cats, two dogs, and
we have two cars in the garage and a pick-up truck. Our children
were even born on the same day, November 22nd, exactly two
years apart. Didn't plan it that way, but the coincidence meant
that they shared every birthday party and grew up almost like
twins. Both our son and daughter scored high academically and
enjoyed a measure of popularity among their peers, perhaps envy.*

*Indeed, our whole family seemed envied by our social circle.
We own our own business. Our large, lovely house is secluded
on nine acres of land with rocky creeks and small waterfalls. This
setting was near perfect for the country-club style of social life
we were living before the 'Big Bang'.*

*This shot, heard around our family's world, occurred in early
February, 1987. Without warning, our daughter, eighteen, tem-
porarily disappeared into the night and we had not the slightest
clue where she had gone. Until we found her safe five days later,
we lived in a hell no religion could invent. She had eloped with a
guy we didn't even know. To this day we don't really know why.
They had fled over the border into South Carolina, a state that
dispenses holy matrimony like barbecued hot-dogs, with few re-
quirements and fewer formalities.*

*During our anguish, our son, Gordon, twenty, travelled home
from college to help look for his sister, Mag. It was during this time
that he chose to tell us that he is gay. Not only that: he announced
that he, too, had been 'married' to a guy for nearly a year.*

*Talk about a double whammy! Our world turned upside-down:
our idyllic existence and our 'Ozzie and Harriet' lifestyle was
forever shattered. But Joyce and I are extremely resilient people.
We believe in the old adage that if life hands you lemons, you
make lemonade. We quickly resolved to pick up the shattered pieces
and make a stained-glass window and I don't mean the sort you
find in churches. I mean the kind of mosaic that exalts diversity
and celebrates family in whatever form.*

*Nothing seemed humorous at the time but a few months later
we began to smile and laugh at the various reactions our friends
and relatives exhibited whenever we told them about 'This Was
the Week that Was'. In one week's time we had discovered that
both our son and our daughter were married to males and that
we had acquired both of these sons-in-law* without having to
pay for either wedding!

*The reactions of our friends and relatives were just as unpre-
dictable as the trajectory of fragments dispersed by the Big Bang.
In some cases, persons we thought would be understanding and
accepting turned out to be anything but, and some of those from
whom we anticipated possible rejection welcomed the new composition of our family with open arms. In a situation like that, it's
easy to find out who your real friends are.*

Dub

Causes

Comfort yourself with the thought
that suffering lays bare the real
nature of things; that is the price
to be paid for a deeper, more truthful
insight into life.

Eugenia Ginzburg

Callers to the helpline ask what causes homosexuality. Our response is 'What would you like to do if we told you the causes?' We ask if they would like to change things, and often they would. When we ask if they would like to change the kind of person their son or daughter is, 'not now' is the regular answer, since usually their child is happier and pleasanter now that they are 'out'.

> *I am coming through the shock of Mark's news a little. I thought I had accepted that he was gay and then after his news found myself saying: Why? If only. . . . Now, following phone calls and your P.F. booklet, not forgetting the prayers, I think I have really accepted the fact. How pertinent the comment in your Parents' Guide: 'If you look for a cause you are wanting a change your child cannot manage. Just accept and love.' How true. I feel I am coping much better now, but it is hard when one is a father alone.*
>
> *Phillip*

Why do parents want to know the causes? Because most of us wish to understand what we've never needed to know about before. We've rarely thought about homosexuality or bisexuality. Non-heterosexuals were from 'somewhere out there' and didn't even appear to have parents – and now we *are* these parents. As parents, we think we have to sort it out, and to work on the causes should surely help us to do this. Yes? Not so!

So, what do we do? We learn more about sexuality – that's the only thing we can do. But what if we don't like what we know? What would you have done if you had known before birth that your child was not heterosexual? Would you have had an abortion? Some would – they tell us so – and really hate their daughter or son now they are out. Why? Is it due to lost expectations?

When you first learned your son or daughter is gay, how did you react? Did you scream, shout and throw things? That's not unusual. Parents react in all sorts of ways. However you acted with your son or daughter, they will have expected it. They will have perhaps heard coming-out stories from friends and have known it might not be plain sailing. They will certainly have known society's attitude to 'those people'.

You might immediately have wondered if it was something you did. Did you bring them up wrongly? Were you to blame in some way? Were you too close, too soft, too disciplined? Should you have forced your son to play football or your daughter to take ballet classes and wear dresses?

No one can make another person's sexuality different to what it is from birth – not you, the parent, not the older lesbian, nor the older gay man. It is no one's fault. No guilt should be attached. It is natural to your gay son or daughter or bisexual child. Does this mean that no research has been done into the causes of homosexuality or bisexuality? You will think there must be a cause and that you, the parent, must take the blame. You feel guilty.

Recent research has been carried out in the USA by Simon LeVay (neuroscientist), Michael Bailey (psychologist) and Richard Paillard (Boston University, School of Medicine). Each has come up with his own findings. LeVay knew he was gay at 12 years old. In 1991, he had the opportunity to scan the brains of 41 cadavers, including 19 homosexual males, and found what many gay people feel to be the case: they are 'born different'. LeVay saw that the hypothalamus (the tiny part of the brain believed to control sexual activity) of those gay males was smaller than that of heterosexual males. However, the results of LeVay's research are suspect since the cause of death in each of the males was HIV/AIDS, and that may have affected the hypothalamus.

Michael Bailey and Richard Paillard were at the same time studying homosexuality in twins, and they published their findings a few months after LeVay. Their results showed that when one of a pair of identical twins is gay, the other is almost three times more likely to be gay than if the twins were fraternal, implying a shared genetic make-up in identical twins. This theory could simply confirm that identical twins are likely to have some make-up in common.

More recently, in 1993, findings in America by Dean Hamer showed that genes from the mother's line may create a gay son's sexuality, leading one mother to say 'At least I can now share some of the blame'. Many mothers, in particular, desperately need to find a cause, in order to take the blame. But even if a gene for homosexuality exists on the x-chromosome, it will still be the case that not all homosexuals have that gene and that not all men with the gene will be homosexual.

The causes of homosexuality are undetermined. Furthermore, none of these findings can be proved. If they could, how would it help us to find causes for bisexuality and lesbianism? They only deal, after all, with gay men.

In speaking to mothers on the helpline, we find that many fathers do the ostrich act, put their heads in the sand: if you don't talk about it, it will go away. Well, here's news: it won't.

Either our children tell or, having bottled it up for so long, sometimes years, they feel they will burst if they cannot tell others. Keeping this secret any longer can lead to illness and they may even consider suicide. Life seems impossible. American research shows one in three gay men or lesbians either attempt or commit suicide. It is little different here in the United Kingdom. It is fortunate when they decide to come out to you, as a loved parent and the one with whom they wish to share this information most of all. For some, the decision to come out at this point is a case of tell or die. They will have struggled long and hard to accept their own sexuality. It is not easy when most of us have been conditioned to believe we are heterosexual. We parents were most likely so conditioned, and we did the same to our children.

If your son or daughter came out to you face to face, it took a lot of courage. If they did it by letter or phone, it was too difficult to do it face to face, or they were too far away. You may have found out 'by accident' – discovered a letter (left perhaps so that you might see it) or overheard a telephone conversation, or you may have been unlucky enough to have an anonymous phone call from some 'kind' person who thought you should know.

Considering that some ten per cent of all society, on average, are gay and that one in every four families has a non-heterosexual member, it really is about time society began to accept that lesbians, gays and bisexuals are everywhere. They are in every walk of life, every village, town, city. They do the most unusual or the most excruciatingly boring jobs, live in large houses, council estates, squats, luxury cruisers or cardboard boxes. They are everywhere, just like heterosexuals. They are not all arty nor do they dress any more oddly or flamboyantly than anyone else.

When you chose to have a baby, you most likely looked into his or her future and planned ahead. You expected certain things to occur at stages in his or her development. We now begin to appreciate that plans cannot always be made so far ahead. We won't always get our own way; parents can be extremely selfish at times.

If you are upset to find your plans askew, you have a right to your feelings of disappointment and despair. You are shocked. No one can be expected to accept a son or daughter coming out immediately. These awful feelings will take their own time, but you can help yourself by trying to re-establish your relationship with your daughter or son, whom you may now see as a stranger. You thought you knew them but you must now set out to relearn. They really are the same person even though at the moment they seem different.

A young Indian living in Calcutta wrote the following letter, which was published some years ago in the magazine *Shakti Khabar* for Asian gays:

Dear Mother,
You love me – I know. Sometimes I just wonder if you love the neighbours a bit more or my Aunt S. For in everything that you do, you seem to be thinking, what will they say? And when you bless me you say, may your father walk proud with head held high because of you. Mother, why don't you ever say 'Be happy'? It's just two words. Be happy!

I don't want to live up to expectations, yours or Grandfather's or the neighbours'. Release me. Don't put that cross around my neck. Let me be not what others want me to be! Don't stunt me with your love; I was not meant to be part of your bonsai garden.

Mother, I know you love me. You buy prawns at outrageous prices to cook me my favourite curry. You love me because I am your son. You carried me for nine months. You love me because I am part of you, and you don't care that I am short or that my nose is kind of snub. You love me because I am you son ... period!

Then when did straight come into the picture? Is a gay son less than a son? Where in the definition of 'son' did 'straight' or 'gay' come in?

Tell me Mother, when you tucked me in to sleep, did you see me as an investment? Tell me, Ma, when you brushed my hair were you prettying me for a daughter-in-law? Is that all I am – a duct through which will pass your grandchildren? Because if I am Ma, I loved you wrong. I loved you because you kept the bogeyman from under my bed. I loved you because whenever I came home from the hostel you'd rustle up some dinner. I loved you – not Mrs R, not the president of the Ladies' Circle.

Ma, I am not asking you to go to Aunt S and say 'Look, this is my son's boyfriend, isn't he smart?' Mother, all I ask is love for me for what I am – your son. Not the boy who won the debate competition, nor the lover of some hairy-legged man. Don't see me through the eyes of Dad's boss or Aunt S. I am not perfect. Somewhere along the way I just got a little bent. But when I was born you had no choice – boy or girl, lame or blind, black-haired or brown-eyed, straight or gay. You only asked for a child.

Accept me as just that, your child. Is that too much to ask, Mother?

With all my love,

Sandip

For you, this new appreciation of your son or daughter is a new beginning, a time to look at people with clarity as individuals, not necessarily as a unit made up of components from each member of that unit, leaving nothing of themselves. Each of us is unique, not a version of our parents or grandparents. We are all different. The mother of a lesbian daughter perfectly illustrates this point:

> *Some time ago my daughter gave me a book. It was called* Different Daughters *and is a collection of pieces by mothers of lesbian daughters.*
>
> *I read it with great interest, was moved by much of the writing, identified with some and not others. At the end I thought: but is my daughter 'different'? She is my daughter and that makes her, to me, infinitely special and infinitely precious.*
>
> *The 'difference' of her sexual orientation is something that means she is a member of a minority group and as such, equally with racial or religious minorities, she is vulnerable to prejudice and I am concerned for her, worry about her and want to protect her from the world.*
>
> *But she is a big girl now. She has learned, sadly sometimes the hard way, to protect herself. She is brave, she is loving and caring, she is creative. She is fortunate in having a wonderful partner and loving and loyal family and friends.*
>
> *Her 'difference' has given her a wider, not narrower, perspective on life and she has taught me and continues to teach me, a great deal. I also enjoy her company enormously.*
>
> *Many other mothers of daughters could, I am sure, say the same. So is Sarah 'different'? Perhaps, yes, and I rejoice in it and am proud of her. But perhaps she is simply, like everyone else's son and daughter, unique!*
>
> *Jenny*

We learn from each experience; otherwise, we cannot move on in our understanding of ourselves, never mind others. You will soon see your child as the worthwhile individual you once thought them. They have not changed, only your perception of them has changed. Your joy in your child will return quite naturally:

It has taken me eight years to come to terms with and get through the trauma of my eldest child being gay.

At first I blamed myself for giving birth to him. My husband still feels terribly guilty but love has conquered in the end. I think to myself, after having counselling, that it is not my fault, it is just the way he developed and what a terrible struggle he must have had to come out. Anyone who can survive living in a world of hate, with mixed race and different sexuality, has great strength.

Peter has settled in a European country because it is quite usual to see gay men and women being together there. I have met some of his gay friends and I couldn't wish my son to have a more charming young man as his partner. So good-looking as well! I gain much comfort in knowing they love each other just as we do and they are prepared to support each other as any married couple would. That makes me happy.

I have had to open my mind to realize this. My son is proud and we are proud of him and for him. Why can't others see our children as worthy? They would gain so much from at least trying to get to know those they chose to hate.

To parents just finding their child is gay: remember that you have lived much longer than they have, so give them a chance to be as they are and live their life freely and without pressure from within the family.

Now I can say I'm so happy to have a gay son, but I know just how much pain there is in the beginning.

                                                    Marian

Feelings of Bereavement and Loss

Life has too many claims and privileges and resources to waste it in lamentations. Let one look forward, not backward.

L. Whiting

The most common word used over the helpline by parents who have just found their son or daughter to be lesbian, gay or bisexual is 'bereaved'. Why bereaved? you might ask. What has this to do with death? The person hasn't even gone away – although for some parents it would have been easier had they already flown the nest.

When I first began taking calls on the Parents' Friend helpline I could not understand the use of such a powerful and final expression. I desperately needed to know why, so took a bereavement counselling course and learned that we suffer numerous losses in a lifetime, from a friend emigrating to a parent remarrying or divorcing; a move to a new area or simply a promotion to an unfamiliar department. These are all life transitions, and finding we have a child whose sexuality is different to what we had thought fits neatly into this category of bereavement.

I also realized that each type of bereavement involves a similar process through which we must pass before reaching the other end of the dark tunnel of despair and loss. That process may be briefly sketched as follows: First comes the *shock* of finding your child is not heterosexual. This is followed by *confusion*. How can this be? Are they mixed up? Perhaps it's a phase and they'll soon be out of it. Third, there is *pain*. How can they do this to us? What have we done to deserve this? Why us? The fourth stage is *anger*. How dare they do this? We hate them! How could we ever think we loved them? It's so dirty. How can we live with this knowledge? It is worth noting here that anger may lead to complete silence on the subject. A parent may become ill by bottling feelings up inside, and depression can result. Do try to talk things through with someone. The final stage is *guilt*. What have we done to cause this? Are we to blame? Perhaps we spoilt her/him. Perhaps we were too strict. It must be our fault. We must be responsible. Where did we fail?

Recognizing and accepting the state of grief helps one to understand and overcome the distress. Some parents progress more quickly than others but patience is required to see each step through fully, so that recovery will be total, whether it be next week, next year or in ten years. Take time to explore your emotions and you'll come through this, not entirely unscathed, but having learned on the way.

I am the mother of Sue and Vick, both lesbians. They came out to me about 12 years ago. Not both together – a few weeks between. Both occasions are clearly pictured in my mind, as if somebody, whoever organizes our lives, stopped the cine-camera for a few frames.

Frame 1: Sue and I were kneeling in front of a glorious fire. 'You said you wanted to talk to me Sue?' She stared at me; it seemed a hard stare with a look of defiance. 'I think I am gay,' she said.

I simply couldn't believe it. She'd had plenty of boyfriends – although she always treated them in a offhand way – but she admittedly, when much younger, used to talk about what kind of wedding she would like. She also had the names ready for her children.

Frame 2: Vick and I were staying with our family in a cottage and sitting by a blazing fire – again! I knew that Vick had been attracted to girls at school and had been concerned about it, but she had boyfriends too. The others had gone out to the pub that evening, and Sue had said, 'Why don't you speak to Vick?' So when they had gone I ventured 'Sue says she is gay'. Vick knelt down in front of me and put her hands on my knees. 'What about you Vick?' But I knew, and started to cry – she held my hands and said, 'Mum, it doesn't matter. . . . I'm all right, I'm happy. . . .

Mum, please *don't be sad, don't worry.'*

And that was it!

My main reaction was shock and utter confusion. I kept say-ing to them and to my husband, 'But I don't understand. . . I don't understand.' I wept and wept. Why was I so devastated? I had worked with a young lesbian and had been fond of her and not in any way judgemental or against gay people. So why was I in such a state? I really don't know why. But I do know that I had hoped and worked all these years to achieve something. To achieve what? I suppose it was to see my daughters settled. And I suppose that meant married, with a good husband who would help create a nest for the next generation. I found the thought that my girls would be reviled by most of society unbearable, and it enraged me. As well as anger, rage, grief and confusion, I felt shame and humiliation. I am not proud of this, but it is true.

We had led a respectable suburban existence: neat school uni-forms, confirmation classes, hairdressing appointments were all part of our family life. Anything tarnishing this image, such as difficulties between my husband and myself, I kept hidden. So my daughters' coming out was a huge blow. What would my friends whose daughters were not gay, think? What about the grandmothers, the aunts and uncles?

I fell into a horrendous, long-lasting depression. I had insom-nia, wept frequently, railed against my husband, wanting to blame him. Why? Why were my girls like this? What had I done wrong?

I rang the Samaritans one night. The chap just listened and said nothing. I rang a gay organization, but the woman on the phone misunderstood me completely so I did not ring again. I went to my doctor: he prescribed anti-depressants, but I thought they would be addictive and was afraid to take them. I went to a university course on sexuality. There was only one other straight person there. All the rest were gay. Although they were nice, kind people, it was not right for me and I was made more and more aware of how gay people are discriminated against.

So what happened? How did I manage to climb out of that depression and become very proud of and happy with my two daughters?

One night I was alone, as I often was, and utterly desperate. I rang a friend who was a member of a reading group to which I belonged. *She guessed that something was wrong, collected two other friends and they came round. They were three good friends and we had met regularly for years. I plucked up my courage and told them my story, which I related in floods of tears. They were very accepting and a great help. One of them called on me every week for many months.*

But eventually what really helped was being accepted on a two-year counselling course, being able to share my experience with fourteen others, and being accepted by them.

It was also outstandingly helpful when a woman I knew told me about her daughter being gay. We had been on a women's group Christmas outing and conversation touched on lesbianism. Outside in the street she told me her daughter was a lesbian and I told her about my daughters. This was a great liberating experience and we wept tears of sadness and joy.

When the counselling course finished I went to join my husband who was working in London. The great mixture of people in central London, where we were living, suited the new me, who was keen to find a life without the restrictions I felt in the suburbs.

I must have spent about five years being depressed, in the wilderness, wasting life. On reflection, if I had found a parent's group straight away I think that would have been a great help and I would have come to terms with the situation and got over the depression much more quickly. Being isolated in secret grief is terrible and to be able to be with people who understand how you feel – that must be so helpful.

I am now very happy and have much to be thankful for. My daughters are women to be proud of. They both do useful work, with particular emphasis on care in the community. They are very close friends and always available to help each other.

Thanks to my daughters and to the people who helped me, I can say that I am a better person than I was twelve years ago.

Pam

What parents tend to forget is that their daughter or son has had a long time to get used to the idea. Parents new to this knowledge are at the point of shock experienced by their child when they found their sexuality to be different to their conditioning. This may have happened years ago. As a new parent you cannot expect to accept this fact immediately. The knowledge must be assimilated and the bereavement process may be worked through to achieve peace within. Your child has been through a similar struggle, through difficult times at school, at home, in opposite-sex relationships. Give yourself time and space to struggle; sometimes the more difficult it seems, the stronger you will be in the end. As you gradually learn to accept that we are all unique, you will also let possessiveness go.

The following advice was sent from the USA by a mother with a gay son; its original source is unknown:

> *To let go doesn't mean to stop caring; it means I can't do it for someone else.*
>
> *To let go is not to cut myself off; it's the realization that I can't control another.*
>
> *To let go is not to enable, but to allow learning from natural consequences.*
>
> *To let go is to admit powerlessness, which means the outcome is not in my hands.*
>
> *To let go is not to try to change or blame another; I can only change myself.*
>
> *To let go is not to care for, but to care about.*
>
> *To let go is not to fix, but to be supportive.*
>
> *To let go is not to judge, but to allow another to be a human being.*
>
> *To let go is not to be in the middle arranging all the outcomes, but to allow others to effect their own outcomes.*
>
> *To let go is not to be protective; it is to permit another to face reality.*
>
> *To let go is not to deny, but to accept.*
>
> *To let go is not to nag, scold or argue, but to search out my own shortcomings and to correct them.*
>
> *To let go is not to adjust everything to my desires, but to take each day as it comes and to cherish the moment.*
>
> *To let go is not to criticize and regulate anyone, but to try to become what I dream I can be.*
>
> *To let go is not to regret the past, but to grow and live for the future.*
>
> *To let go is to fear less and love more.*

*

*My cousin passed the Parents' Friend booklet on to me and I
found it so helpful, after struggling for so long alone.*

*Seven years ago Gerard, who is now 26, told me he was gay.
He expected to be thrown out. My husband would have done
this, but I managed, though deeply shocked, to say I was always
here and Gerard would always have a home with us. My main
upset at the time was that he had been unable to communicate
with us and I hadn't realized we had grown so distant. He was
always independent and, at times, offhand, but I put it down to
unhappiness at school where he had insisted he stay to take A
Levels.*

*My husband still rejects Gerard and, although he will see him
on neutral ground, talking with him fairly openly, has never
mentioned his lifestyle. He will not meet the partner with whom
Gerard has now lived for five years. I am left in the middle trying to hold together a family which is my life. I love them all
dearly. My daughter is married and her husband accepts Gerard's
lifestyle and they have all visited him and his partner, whereas,
when Gerard and Colin come here, my husband refuses to see
them. This hurts so much as this is 'home' to all my family.*

*Gerard has now said he will not come to any family occasion
without Colin. They have both now been invited to a family chris-
tening and my husband says he will not be present if Gerard and
Colin are there together.*

*My own brother and family all accept, if they do not entirely
agree with, Gerard's situation.*

*My husband says it is worse than bereavement as the way he
feels is so final. I am very relieved at the moment that Gerard has
found happiness but it has left his mother desperately unhappy,
which he does not realize. I only hope he stays in the relationship
with Colin, who is such a likeable young man. My husband is
missing so much!*

Irene

Often the parent who cannot fully accept or understand the
child is the one who chooses not to look for help. We find
from experience it is often the father who finds it most difficult and who buries his head; he could learn much simply by

asking for help and searching for some way of understanding his child's sexuality.

Some of the grief a parent feels has to do with lost expectations. A mother may say she is sad her son won't have children. When asked if she has checked whether her son indeed wants children, her response is often 'No'. So, we ask, whose expectations are being affected? Some lesbian, gay or bisexual people will wish for a family of their own, just as some heterosexuals will choose not to have a family. It is a matter of choice.

Parents with bisexual children may state that they feel less grief when their son or daughter has a partner of the opposite gender, since then it looks as if they could marry, and that is easier to accept, more comfortable. But those expectations are not always realized. It is important to try to accept your bisexual child's partner of whatever gender. Each relationship deserves validation.

Seeking Advice

> *I am pleased to say that the relationship between myself and my son is wonderful. He and his friends have, and still are, educating me as to their way of life, the difficulties and prejudices. The majority of gay and lesbian people I have met appear very happy and loving people.*
>
> *Janine*

When your son or daughter came out to you, your reaction may have been dishonest. Many parents who ring the helpline tell of accepting the news calmly, making all the right noises and appearing to say exactly the 'right things'. But the way they feel is far removed from the impression they gave. They feel lost. There are many questions to ask, but their child has gone off thinking all is well at home, while their parents' world has been turned upside-down.

Often, once out, the lesbian, gay or bisexual child will not stay around long enough for the inquisition. Those who live at home may clam up, not wishing to go further into the subject. Those non-heterosexual daughters and sons who offer to answer any questions are perhaps the ones to help parents most at the beginning. This is how many parents find the Parents' Friend telephone number; many daughters and sons plan their 'coming-out day' carefully, ensuring support not only for themselves but for their parents also. We regularly have calls from those ready to come out, asking how we deal with 'new' parents and what we are likely to say. Satisfied, they go away with easy minds knowing they can safely give our number to their parents.

Giving your child the message 'I'm OK – you're OK' when you are not, can cause problems later. One daughter rang the helpline, devastated. She had a very good first reception on telling her mother and went away happy to know how open-minded her mother was. Six years later she found, from speaking with an aunt, that her mother was still upset.

When your child comes out, you may feel so ill that you visit your GP. Some doctors will be able to explain how natural it is to be gay; others will have no knowledge whatsoever about homosexuality, and bisexuality, especially, will defeat them. Some doctors will offer pills to calm you and to help you to sleep, but this is not what you want. Information is the best panacea – a leaflet or some literature on homosexuality or bisexuality. But there is little available. Nothing seems to encourage doctors to become educated on the subject in order to help devastated parents. Some parents even speak of suicidal feelings after seeing the doctor, as they had expected some comfort.

Why do GPs show ignorance on sexuality? Doctors are trained to treat illness with pills and potions and expect to see improvement or cure. No one can, in fact, 'treat' sexuality, as it is part of each one of us. We are born with it. Neither homosexuality nor bisexuality is an illness to be treated or 'cured'.

What *is* sexuality then? If your GP knows little, perhaps your priest or minister will be able to help? Perhaps, but not necessarily. Many do not see this as a spiritual matter. However, different churches will deal with their acceptance of non-heterosexuality according to how they interpret their Bible or other teachings. Some churches are totally against lesbian, gay or bisexual people. Spiritual leaders have been known to instruct parents to turn their child out of the home unless he or she changes and, as we have seen, this is an impossibility for our non-heterosexual children. How caring is this way of thinking?

It is fair to admit that some GPs are wonderful, often giving good education along with our telephone number. And ministers of religion are not always naïve, though fewer seem to know about Parents' Friend or any other parents' organization. Please do not be put off trying them, but remember that you are opening your heart to someone who may know little about the subject and who may be antagonistic to non-heterosexual persons, in spite of their nominally caring position in the community. If they fail to sympathize with you, remember that for someone to empathize, usually they will have had to 'be there' themselves.

So, trust your parent contacts, unless they tell you your son's or daughter's sexuality is unacceptable and wrong – some will do this. (These are so-called religious 'helplines'.) Any number obtained through Parents' Friend will be for a safe and caring helpline or contact.

Fortunately, often through complicated routes, parents will find the telephone numbers of helplines or parent contacts who will provide support, comfort, understanding and honest answers to their many questions.

A mother explains her need to educate herself even after eight years of knowing her son is gay:

> *It is about eight years since my son wrote to say he was worried he might be homosexual. I tried to talk to him about this and found out what made him think this was so. He had just completed his university course, gained a good degree, and was about to move to another course in a different city.*
>
> *He is now fully qualified and his job is at risk due to the recession. In all that time I have never again had the opportunity to talk to him about his sexuality. At the beginning I tried to put him in touch with a counsellor but he did nothing about it and I was disappointed at the time. Looking back, I feel now he thought I was trying to 'cure' his homosexuality, which was not the case at all. I felt he needed some help to understand his sexuality and I was worried about him – on his own and in a big city, with unsolved and probably unsolvable problems.*
>
> *I am so very afraid about the prejudice against homosexuality, particularly since AIDS is still seen as a 'gay' disease. His friends seem to be drawn from the gay community but he has not yet formed a close relationship. I constantly worry about him. I realize I need to learn far more about homosexuality, and then I may understand my son better – I love him so.*
>
> *Betina*

Should you ring the Parents' Friend helpline for advice, we never fail to say that we do not give advice. But we know from our own experience that to be able to talk to someone who understands, who has also 'been there' is affirming of our devastation and supportive of us as hurting individuals, who are in need of all the help other caring parents can pass on. To be able to meet in a group is even better.

Once you find a parents' helpline or contact, you will be able to ring when you are feeling down and in need of someone to listen to your fears and worries. You may also come to the stage where you will wish to share your good times in having a non-heterosexual daughter or son. We will rejoice with you.

Parental Acceptance

Few individuals consider the issue of sexuality when they decide to have a baby, or at their child's birth. Most parents of non-heterosexuals are heterosexual and will rarely have been educated to appreciate alternative sexualities. We are conditioned to believe we are heterosexual and feel the same must be true of all other people.

Many children first hear of those who are not heterosexual through whispered asides, which indicate that there is something not quite right about non-heterosexuals. This evasiveness and lack of concrete information only invites further curiosity. The negative vibes are clearly picked up. From an early age children learn it must be wrong to be different. This leaves them little space to feel good about themselves if they realize that they too, are 'one of them'. They feel unacceptable and isolated. Heterosexual parents should not blame themselves for a lack of education on the subject due to conditioning, but it does not help conditioned offspring to feel good about themselves. The following letters all come from parents who have learned to accept, in varying degrees, their children's sexuality.

It's now over two years since our son broke the news to us that he was gay. Not the best time – Mother's Day! There have been many tears since but we are a close family, and much discussion has helped us.

We have met his partner and together they have been to our home for the day. We all got on fine, but my wife and I would find it so difficult to stay overnight with them and it seems that our visits would now be only for the day.

Eric

Eric and his wife are not alone in being unable to stay in the same house (or under the same roof) as their gay child and partner. For some parents of unmarried heterosexuals it is equally difficult. This is often the most difficult situation to overcome. Eventually, however, parents find it acceptable or can, at least, close the bedroom door and forget it.

> *It is only by easy stages that one learns to accept a gay child. It is a stony road but how much harder for your own to gain the courage to come out. I'm glad I have a strong faith but I felt so frozen and on my own. I was still coming to terms with the loss of my husband when my first numbed response was: 'I don't think it can ever change our relationship' – thank goodness! But was I glad my son suggested I might like to read the Parents' Friend booklet. I felt so ignorant but found comfort knowing there were others facing the same trauma.*
>
> *The first time I met my son's partner was an anxious hurdle, but better, of course, than I'd expected and now I'm happily at ease – after all, they always wash up after a meal!!! Can't complain about that.*
>
> *It's a gradual, acclimatizing relationship. As a parent, I beg of you: please don't close your heart – your own need your love even more now.*
>
> *Patience*

When a child first comes out to a parent, a 'stranger' may suddenly appear in his or her place. Yet it is not the child who has changed, it is the parents' perception of the child that has changed. A newly out gay person can take on an energy up to then unknown, and seem to go 'over the top' in their behaviour – visiting as many gay pubs and clubs as possible and staying out till all hours, or not coming home at all. This can greatly upset a parent already struggling with the news.

At Parents' Friend, we tell parents that newly out sons and daughters have a lot of lost time to make up for – time spent hiding from the world. They may feel they have a lost childhood to experience. Gay people tell us they have never felt so happy or so free, and they rejoice in their new-found pride in themselves. Usually, they become less extrovert with the passage of time.

Easter 1991: Stephen had cooked us a lovely meal – Chinese, every-
body's favourite – but before we'd eaten even one mouthful he
announced he was gay!

I felt at that moment and even for a long time afterwards as
though our world had ended. Jim and I looked at each other in
disbelief. Stephen was still talking about how he'd known since
he was fourteen but hadn't wanted to believe it himself. He spoke
of how unhappy he'd been and how now at nineteen, after his
second term at university he'd decided to come out.

The meal was never eaten. Nothing in life had prepared us for
this. Stephen had always seemed a normal, quite masculine, boy,
sensitive and artistic, popular with his own group of friends and
occasional girlfriends – though no one serious.

The next few days were very difficult. Jim went to work but he
hadn't been sleeping and the worry lines were etched on his face.
We'd cried together that first night, lost in our thoughts and
unable to put our feelings into words. At the time it felt as though
we'd lost Stephen altogether. The grief seemed unbearable and I
didn't think life would ever be the same again. Suddenly I felt
awkward with my own son. It was as though I no longer knew
him. I tried desperately hard not to think what this other side of
his life involved.

I quickly discovered there are no magazines on the subject, no
books to buy, no one I felt I could talk to. Our families live away
so we have no one close by and I doubt I'd have wanted to tell
anyone. I felt very alone at the time. After the first couple of
nights Jim seemed resigned to Stephen's gayness and didn't want
to talk. He had pushed it all to the back of his mind. In contrast,
I was worrying away at it and thinking that if I knew more per-
haps I could help Stephen to change.

During those Easter holidays Stephen's pride in his gayness
seemed to grow and he couldn't understand why we were finding
it so difficult to accept, but he was also sad that he'd caused us
pain and he had a real and obvious need to be reassured of our
love. My message to him seemed to be 'We love you but . . .' and
I realize now that that was wrong. It wasn't just another fad.

He told me how he'd been going to gay clubs and how he'd
been battling with his homosexuality all his teenage years, and
all the time just wanting to be like the other lads. He'd suffered

great emotional pain seeing the prejudices people feel against gays and says he'd even contemplated suicide rather than admit to being homosexual.

How could we as parents have missed all this unhappiness, not seen the signs? The Easter holidays eventually came to an end and we said a restrained goodbye to Stephen. For the first time ever, I was glad to see him go. We didn't talk much about Stephen and his gayness, but it was always there and my tears were never far away. We'd decided not to tell Stephen's sister for the time being as she was on her final run-down to GCSEs and we thought it better to leave it.

The turning point for me was the day I walked into our local charity shop and there, amongst all the odds and ends, was a roll of quite old magazines for sale. There, right on top of the outside cover of a magazine for spring 1988, were the words 'My Son Is Gay'. I handed over my 10p and hastily tucked the roll of magazines into my bag, hoping no one would see those glaring words and know why I'd bought the magazines! Once home I couldn't wait to start reading and it was like an awakening. Here was someone else with my problem, the same heartache and turmoil. I read it over and over and knew I'd reached a turning point. I felt that in the magazine I had found a friend, another mother suffering as I was – but her problems seemed to be, quite unbelievably, worse than mine.

I eventually heard about Parents' Friend. I sent for leaflets and a book and began to realize, through these, that my world hadn't come to an end after all and that, although we were saddened by Stephen's gayness, we could learn to understand and accept it.

My thoughts on Stephen's gayness can change from day to day. I try to be positive about it but, sometimes, the old despair creeps back. Stephen eventually told his sister and she took it in her stride. She said it made no difference to her and I'm sure it hasn't. I couldn't honestly say it made no difference to Jim and me. The night Stephen told us he was gay, all our hopes and dreams for him seemed to die for ever. Suddenly there were so many new things to think about. The worry over AIDS, how his homosexuality would affect his future career and, for me, the sadness that he'd probably never know the same married happiness that Jim and I have enjoyed.

I know that it is our fear of rejection that stops us telling family and friends and that, because of this, Stephen feels that he can't be his true self. Stephen and I have talked about coming out and I sometimes think it would be better if we did, but I know that things once said can never be unsaid, and so we leave it.

If, one day, Stephen meets someone he wants to spend his life with, I should hope that we could welcome that person into our family as Stephen's chosen partner. In the meantime, Stephen knows we love him very much and that we'd always support him should the need arise. We do hope that that knowledge will help to keep him happy.

                                                                    Lorna

Adopted children and their parents can face additional pressures:

On initially hearing the news from our son when he phoned to tell us – I was in the house alone at the time – my first reaction was a shocked acceptance, the most overwhelming feeling being compassion for our son, who was very upset. He too was on his own at the time and away from home. All my hopes and dreams for his future fell into a heap and I seemed to pass through a gate into a life I knew little about, a life I felt contained loneliness, worry, unhappiness and secrecy for our son and unacceptability to the world at large.

When my husband came home later he rang our son to re-assure him of our love and support only to find that he had also phoned his sisters that same evening to tell them. Both our daughters were upset, for our son, for us, and for themselves, but gave their brother their love and support.

We decided the best way to help would be to do something positive, find out as much as we could about homosexuality. We phoned our local hospital, explained the situation and made an appointment with a nursing sister who was involved with the local gay community and dealt with general sexual problems. She turned out to be a lovely lady, near to retirement, who helped us such a lot. We then told our close family members and two trusted sets of friends.

We are in our fourth year of knowing and now realize what a terrible burden it must have been for our son to carry his secret on his own. Happily he knows that if he wants to he can talk to us about his friends and partner and we have met a couple of them when they stayed with us on weekend visits and we had friendly times together.

One of my worries is not being able to be open and just say 'Our son is gay and it makes no difference to us'. I hate the secrecy and having to evade so much, but we feel we must for our son's sake, because of the prejudice he may receive. Maybe we are wrong in this.

I must say that since knowing more about homosexuality and belonging to Parents' Friend, my husband and I are better people and have been given a new dimension to our lives. I know I now give much more thought and have greater understanding of the complexity of the human condition and human nature and I do not judge situations as perhaps I may have done previously.

I would just like to add that our own son has an additional problem to cope with – that he is adopted, and now, being in his mid-twenties, is feeling a deep sense of 'biological loss' and lone-liness. He has to cope with not having any natural roots and knowing that he will never have a natural family of his own. He is receiving counselling for this. He also had to pluck up courage a second time to tell us, his adoptive parents, that he feels the need to trace his birth parents. He knows that he has our support in this and can talk to us about it. My husband and I now find ourselves in the rather strange position of hoping against hope that our son will find, be accepted by, and, if possible, enjoy a happy relationship with, his birth parents. The only thing that is important to us is that he can find a bit more peace of mind and some happiness. Our greatest fear for him is rejection. Meeting natural parents is such a big thing to do, emotionally, for the child and the natural parents and, more often than not, does not have a fairy-tale ending, we know.

Barbara

It is not uncommon for there to be two or more non-hetero-sexual children in a family, but no one has yet researched sufficiently to produce a satisfactory explanation. One mother with a gay son informed her lesbian daughter with a smile that it's easier the second time around. The following letter seems to echo this idea.

> *I am the mother of four young adults, two daughters and two sons. For the last five years I have known that one of my daughters and one of my sons are gay. I can say that quite happily and acceptably now but – just to recap the time that my youngest daughter stunned me with the news that she is gay. At that time I was still coming to terms with the divorce from their father, my two eldest youngsters had left home and I was learning to cope with life as a single parent with two teenagers. I had absolutely no idea whatsoever that this situation was going to crop up in my family.*
>
> *Although taken completely by surprise, I hugged my daughter and reassured her of my everlasting love, while trying to fight back the turmoil inside me. I had a lot to learn and when I felt able to discuss it with her I gradually reaccepted her into my life as she was, not how I'd always thought her to be. This seemed to be an essential part of the 'moving on' process.*
>
> *During this time of readjustment, my eldest son also told me his news. He was 23 at the time and later said he just felt he could tell me when he saw the positive reaction his sister had received. In his case, it certainly explained a few puzzles to me. He had suffered badly at school and didn't seem interested in girls, which I put down to the fact that he just hadn't met any he liked! We drew together closely as a family through all this and talked a lot. Their father didn't really take it seriously and still doesn't, so he isn't a support to me but I am now in a long-term relationship with someone who has been an enormous support right from the beginning and has helped me such a lot.*
>
> *Maybe I will never completely understand, but I will keep on listening, loving and learning, with God's help.*
>
> *Rachel*

Rachel now acts as a parent contact.

It is amazing how often parents will disown a child once he or she has come out. But it is also encouraging to know that most parents eventually come round, and feel a strong need to understand as much as possible. They acknowledge a desperate urge to educate themselves and so support their child.

In addition, many, through their new understanding of prejudice and discrimination against non-heterosexuals, choose to become telephone contacts, or at least open allies of all oppressed groups of people. Having a non-heterosexual child teaches parents a great deal about minorities.

This weekend our son, Adam, and his partner have celebrated their ninth anniversary.

It can sometimes be a problem in finding the appropriate card for them as most wedding anniversary cards have a female and male image portrayed, but if we look carefully we can usually find a suitable one for them. If anyone had told me nine years ago that we would be helping our son celebrate an anniversary of marriage to another man I would have had them committed!!!

When Adam told me that he was gay I felt as if my world had crashed around me. I'm ashamed to say that I rejected him for a couple of months until someone (thank God) pointed out that unless I 'got my act together' I would lose him.

With the support of my husband and daughter I did 'get my act together' and started to think very seriously about my future relationship with Adam. I realized that above all else I loved my son and that the only thing that had changed was that now we knew more about him than ever before and that we were privileged in this fact. Also I realized just how much he must have suffered before he came out and how brave he was to do so.

About two years after my personal 'bombshell' exploded I was able to be totally accepting of my son's sexuality and Gordon and I founded 'ACCEPTANCE', a helpline and support organization for the parents and families of lesbians and gay men. By listening and talking to parents who are distressed and confused we can empathize fully with their feelings and those of their children.

Our work has led us to make contact with so many lovely people here and abroad and we know that through our lesson of acceptance we have been able to help hundreds of parents and families over the last seven years.

We can honestly say that we don't regard our son as 'being gay'. He's just Adam, our son, whom we love and with whom we have a wonderful relationship.

Jill

*

When I spoke to you recently I desperately needed support. My son had come out to me the previous week when I visited him.

When he asked to talk to me, terrible thoughts had me worried sick. So when he said he was gay, I heard the news with some relief. I seemed to do and say all the right things and even invited him and his partner to join me for a meal, where the ice was broken.

I was shocked by the unexpected disclosure and felt quite emotional. I spent the whole night writing down my thoughts and my love for him. I posted it as I walked to the railway station the following morning.

He had asked me to break the news to his father, which I did the following evening. He was terribly upset, especially that we had not been aware earlier when we would perhaps have been able to ease his worry.

Lily

It is never easy for a parent to be informed of a child's gayness, but finding out more than one child is gay can be a terrible bombshell. Fathers tend to find it particularly difficult to deal with the information, and are the ones most likely to clam up. Robert's method of coping with knowing both his daughters are lesbian is therefore all the more admirable. Also, when a marriage is fragile, it can be shattered instantly by such a revelation. **Robert** and **Pat** found their marriage threatened in this way, until a solution arose and provided them with a second chance.

In late 1981 I learned from my wife, Pat, that our two daughters, Sue and Vick, had told her they were lesbians.

I am a professional manager, had been working long hours and was away from home all week. There were problems between Pat and me at the time.

The full impact did not register with me immediately. I was too taken aback by what I had learned. Life became something of a blur which I cannot fully recall. For Pat, it was far, far, worse. She was on her own in our home, dark and gloomy in the winter, all the time pouring with rain or surrounded by mist, or so it seemed.

Pat almost went out of her mind. She seemed to withdraw into herself and did not want to meet friends. But eventually she booked on to a two-year training course for counsellors which helped her to get a better understanding of how to deal with the matters that were so affecting our lives. This course saved our sanity and probably our marriage.

As time went on we told others – relatives, friends – that our daughters were lesbians. Sometimes we spoke in anger, sometimes with diffidence, but as we realized that they were not judgemental we found ourselves better able to live with our daughters' sexuality.

We have now been able to establish a great relationship with our daughters, see them reasonably often and talk on the telephone frequently. We love them and we know that they love us.

Now twelve years later, Pat and I are happier together than we have ever been. I have retired from work and we do a lot together. We are relaxed about our daughters' sexuality – not always happy, but accepting – and, we hope, understanding. As they are content with their lives, we are also.

Parents Coming Out to Others

I suspected for a long time that Carl was gay but it is 'something else' when your fears are confirmed.

I decided that I would have to tell my husband. My heart went out to my son when I realized he must have kept his secret for years and I couldn't keep the secret from my husband for two weeks, as my son had asked me to do.

My husband was devastated when I told him, but with all the knowledge I had from the Parents' Friend booklet I was able to persuade him that it wasn't the end of the world, that at long last our son was really happy.

Whilst his father accepts the situation and is still on the same friendly terms as he always has been, he is not yet ready to meet Carl's gay friend. He does say he will be able to do this in time, but not just yet as it is so new at the moment.

Carl was extremely open with us and answered all my questions. I am soon going to meet some of his gay friends and really look forward to it. Carl tells me they are lovely caring people and very supportive of one another.

I still get waves of depression now and again, but it's not because my son is gay. I simply can't help worrying what the future will hold for him. Still, I know I must let him go and allow him to live his own life. I really will try.

*

When my son was about 18 months old he was running across the living room when he turned and smiled at me and, in a flash, I knew he was gay! This may seem strange to other parents and I know they will find it difficult to accept, but that's the way it was. I just knew. I never told anyone, not even my husband. I kept it to myself and suppose you could call it a mother's intui-

tion. When Phillip was nearly 18 he told me himself. I passed the 'news' on to my own mother and her response was 'Never mind dear, it might go away'. Even when I told her it wouldn't, she always believed it would disappear overnight.

I joined Parents' Friend some time ago and am so pleased I did. In spite of knowing of my son's gayness for such a long period of time, it has given me strength to be part of the group. This I didn't have before when dealing with other people and I would now urge anyone with a gay child to join a group like this.

My prayer is always that the world's attitude to gay people changes and that society can begin to see our children for the lovely people that they are.

Emily-Rose

You may have guessed your daughter or son's secret but when it was confirmed to you, your feelings changed. You may have coped before it was made fact, but now find it incredibly difficult and wonder why. You may have hoped in the beginning that it was a phase and would go away – even looked to the day when this might happen.

*

My emotions on learning for sure that my son is gay have varied from day to day. Mark now actually talks with me. I'm still finding everything very difficult to understand, but things are improving from day to day. Talking with him puts my emotions back on an even keel.

Not knowing for certain for several years probably helped in some ways. I went through all the wide range of emotions before Mark confirmed he was gay – anger, denial, bereavement – just a few to mention. Mark will have my love and support always. I've told him this.

Mandy

*

My son did not have to tell me he was gay. Instinctively I guessed and my world fell apart. I simply could not accept this.

My son and I were so close. How could he? My whole being reacted against it. How could I possibly protect him now? I was quite complacent about my love for him; I took it for granted, but suddenly things had changed. I could not, now, I thought, hold him up to the world and say 'Look at him – look at this beautiful boy I have made.' Suddenly I was ashamed, terrified. People would find out, point fingers.

I got drunk a lot then, and when I was drunk I cruelly attacked my child. I said vile things to him and he had nobody to turn to.

He found Parents' Friend for me.

I enjoyed the meetings. It was wonderful to meet other parents who felt much as I did. I could identify with most of them, but still, deep down, I could not accept it.

My son was a bright child and I had always been so proud of him. Now he seemed to have spoiled it all. I behaved like a spoiled child whose goodies had been confiscated. Then, about three years ago, my son had moved away to begin his career in another city and I was waiting for him to arrive home for the weekend. I believe it was God – for who else could have changed me? I was filled with the old love I thought I had lost for ever. It did not matter any longer if people knew. He was still the same boy, lovable, kind, caring and gentle. It was such a wonderful and overwhelming rush of relief and love. I told him I had come to terms, at last, with his sexuality. He was so surprised and told me he'd thought I'd come to terms with it a long time before.

It seemed my love had, once more, settled down to being unconditional and I am now, again, a truly happy, lucky and proud mother of my gay son.

Jeanne

Parents who guess their daughter's or son's sexuality will, perhaps, still go through the grieving process in the same way as those parents who had no idea. It is possible for each of us to learn to understand, accept and feel fine about our children's sexuality. But it is normal to wonder if you'll ever recover from the trauma you're experiencing, and to be uncertain how to share the news with other members of the family, let alone friends.

Let us look at siblings first. Should they be told? When are they old enough to know? Remember that your son says he knew 'for ever', or your daughter realized she was 'different' at five years old! Many children feel they don't 'fit', but can't say why until their bodies begin to change at puberty, and they acknowledge their attraction to members of their own gender.

When younger children ask questions, including the usual ones about where babies come from, answer them honestly and without embarrassment. Your son may not be your only gay child; your lesbian daughter may already know her older sister is also lesbian but has never dared tell you. It is useful to remember that on average one in every four families has a gay member, though this number is not necessarily evenly distributed over the population.

What about grandparents? Are they really too old to understand? It is an individual choice, but some grandparents are more able to support their grandchildren than parents, since they have more time and patience to explore the surrounding feelings.

Do you tell friends? If you don't mind losing some, then go ahead. Some won't want to understand; others may turn against you. But you will learn who your friends are. At the very least, your openness will give others a chance to test their prejudices and decide to learn more about the subject.

Whatever you decide, first of all you must confer with your son or daughter. It is not for you to tell the world if she or he prefers to take it gently. Your child should be allowed to decide who may or may not be told. Some gay sons or daughters will be so relieved to have abandoned the burden of living two lives that they will approve your telling anyone. But even then, they may choose that certain people are not told. It is important to respect their wishes. It is their sexuality at issue, and this is very personal.

John is still living with his friend and seems so happy now. We all hope this will continue. My two daughters have been wonderful in their support, as have been their partners. The men have not yet met John's friend but we met Bryan recently and he's a very nice person. John is 25 soon, so we said we would take them both – with our daughters and their partners – to the theatre and a meal.

We have told no other members of our families about John and Bryan's relationship – they think they are just buddies – as their

*attitudes to gay people leave a lot to be desired. I feel I just couldn't
cope with them just now.*

   *John is to be an usher at his younger sister's wedding, as he
was with his other sister, and we are hoping the day will go well.
We just cannot bring ourselves to invite Bryan to the wedding
because of the pressure on us from other members of both families. John finds this very hard to understand and I really wish
we were brave enough, but we simply cannot do it.*

                                                                          Pam

If you feel you will never be able to tell anyone, you should
respect your feelings. Eventually, you may feel more relaxed
and occasionally find yourself telling someone. This will show
how you have moved on: 'Never' is a long time.

If you speak to other parents with non-heterosexual offspring,
you will begin to feel more comfortable when friends ask if
your son has a girlfriend or if your daughter is married yet.
There are helplines and contacts all over the country and, if
there is a group meeting locally, then there will be opportunities to meet parents face to face. Either way, you will be
able to speak in total confidence to someone who has 'been
there' and understands the sort of emotions that surround the
discovery that your daughter or son is lesbian, gay or bisexual.

You can begin to educate yourself by reading sensible books
on the subject. The best ones are written by lesbian, gay or
bisexual people themselves, or by parents with lesbian, gay or
bisexual offspring. I am suspicious of those books by people
who *think* they know how we feel. Such feelings can never be
verbalized by someone who has not experienced the emotions.

*When an unmarried daughter or son comes to you and says, 'Can
I speak to you privately?', the first thought is, 'My God, she's
pregnant'; or 'My God, he's made some girl pregnant!' and we
have been geared to thinking that this is the most traumatic thing
that caring parents will have to contend with.*

   *How different when the daughter or son says, 'Mum, I'm gay'
and it suddenly dawns that this is the one thing that you were
never taught about. Where do you begin? How can you hope to
advise about or even understand homosexuality; it has always*

been some obscure word, some alien thing.

Then come the recriminations: 'Where did I go wrong?' 'Why didn't I notice that he (or she) was growing up differently to his or her sisters and brothers?' 'Am I a potential lesbian or my husband a potential gay?' 'Should I have insisted on her (or him) being more athletic instead of sitting reading so much?' So many questions, so few answers.

Now I'd like to take up my own story in the hope that whoever reads it may find some comfort and help if they have a gay son or daughter. I have a lesbian daughter in her 30s, a heterosexual son in his 20s and a heterosexual daughter in her early 20s, but I will speak only about my elder daughter.

Linda did all the usual things one expects a child to do. She was a very good pupil, gaining recognition in most of her school subjects. Perhaps if we'd been a little more aware we might have noticed that Linda was very lonely. I don't mean she didn't have friends. On the contrary, she had lots of friends and was often sought out by other girls as someone who would find time to listen to their problems. In spite of this, however, she was always a loner.

I suppose we'd noticed the absence of boyfriends but put it down to Linda being so involved with everything that was going on in college that she didn't have time for much social life.

On leaving college she had various jobs, battling with being told she was over-qualified. One job was in an antique shop, working for two lesbians, but this didn't worry me unduly as I'd seen no sign that Linda was unsure about her own sexuality. I did wonder, however, whether they would try to make her a lesbian but she told me that lesbians weren't made, they just are.

I'd always brought my children up to accept everyone for what they are and not for what we expect them to be. I was totally unprepared when, in the midst of a party, she said 'Can I speak to you privately?' Although I didn't think she was going to tell me she was pregnant, I really had no idea what she was going to say. I only knew it was important as we have the type of friends who share in our troubles and happinesses as we do theirs, and the fact that it couldn't be said in front of others showed how important it must be to Linda.

Once in the bedroom Linda told me she was a lesbian and told me that the young woman with her was her lover. I was completely

*dumbfounded. Thoughts went flashing through my mind about
the number of times this problem had arisen when I worked for the
Samaritans. People would ring to say their son or daughter had
come out to them and I'd thought my sympathetic approach and
clinical answers were all that were needed. How wrong I was.
Now it was happening to me and why didn't all those answers seem
to fit my own situation? Then, for a moment I stopped thinking
about me as I realized just what it had cost Linda to tell me. Yes,
she knew I'd usually defend my children against any prejudice
but this was something that would affect all the family in some way.
Looking at her face I was ashamed that I'd hesitated to reassure her.*

*I said I'd telephone her brother and sister and tell them, which
I did, only to be told 'Didn't you know? We guessed a long time
ago.' Having overcome this first obstacle I thought: now for the
friends! I knew I couldn't go from one to the other telling them
individually so I decided to tell them all at once.*

*Feeling I was putting my friendships through the most rigor-
ous test I'd ever had to do, I went downstairs to the party, turned
the music down and said I had something important to tell my
visitors . . . and I told them all that Linda had just told me she
was gay. I then said that if anyone wanted to leave I'd quite
understand. The concern my friends showed, not just for me and
my younger daughter and son, but for Linda too, was incredible.
Some had guessed but weren't absolutely sure.*

*After that day I felt I was much more able to cope. When I
would hear people talking about homosexuals, as though it were
a dirty word, I'd remember I had the support of friends and wouldn't
feel so hurt.*

*Once Linda came out I spent the next year finding out every-
thing I could about lesbians and gays. It was then I realized just
how ignorant we all are about alternative lifestyles. I also discovered how anxious gay people are to teach us about their lives
– if only we show an interest.*

*Then I began to think about other parents and to wonder how
they were coping on hearing those words 'Can I speak to you privately?'
Eventually, after many obstacles were overcome I started a helpline
for those who, like myself, found they had lesbian or gay children.*

*Linda suggested I go along to the London Lesbian and Gay
Centre to talk with some of her friends and I thought this a good*

idea until I realized my ex-husband and I would be the odd ones out. It was a very traumatic experience, as we had no idea of what to expect. We needn't have worried as we were made to feel we belonged right from the start. Some of the young people there greeted us with a kiss and hugs as though they simply couldn't believe that parents would be interested in visiting a gay club.

I will always be grateful to my younger daughter and my son during the first few weeks of running the helpline. The times I started to cook dinner at five and eventually served it at eight were numerous. The helpline calls were all-absorbing.

On 16th February 1988 I was asked to speak in the House of Commons on behalf of parents like myself with a lesbian daughter or gay son. Who would ever have thought that Eve, the mother from the council estate, would be able to do this? Not I. But I am so grateful now for my lesbian daughter who helped me to be in a position to go out and educate myself to such an extent that I had the courage to appear at Westminster.

Eve

*

I have been happily married for 34 years; our family consists of three sons and one daughter.

Tom, our youngest, is nearly 25 and lives and works in Amsterdam with his partner, Jan, and it was Tom who flew home in November 1992 to tell us he is gay. We thought our world had collapsed. There was a lot of kissing and hugging but much heartache and many tears. (I don't think I stopped crying for a month.) Three days later Tom returned and we tried to stop the weeping and wailing and understand. Our daughter, who was the only member of the family 'in the know' was a great help with her very enlightened attitude. We talked endlessly, blaming ourselves for the fact he was gay. I'd wanted another girl when he was expected and other, equally irrational, reasons came to mind.

We felt guilty that having thought we were so close to this son, we had not been aware of his unhappiness at 16. At the same time we felt resentful that having kept his secret all these years, he had finally told us! We wished we hadn't known, thought we'd never be happy again.

Believing we had a very liberal outlook, we found it a shock to realize our thinking was based upon such shaky foundations. (We would have been totally accepting of your son or daughter, but it was different when it was our own.) I'm ashamed to say, the problems this knowledge created for us were our chief concern. Would it split the family and lose us friends?

A vicar we knew through working with his wife said it was 'no big deal'; at the time, I thought 'That's all he knows'! This encouraged us to tell the three couples we were especially friendly with and they too were supportive, as we had hoped, and really expected, since they were all very fond of Tom.

Somehow we had a good family Christmas, though Tom was not with us as he was, and still is, working abroad.

In March of this year we invited Tom to bring his partner, a young Dutchman, over for a visit. Preparing for this visit was a very difficult time for us. The crying had more or less stopped, but our wine bill (and I suspect our blood pressures) shot up! We decided to treat them as we did our other children in a committed relationship, though my husband and I nearly fell out over this.

'The day' arrived and we soon realized we were very lucky that Jan was an extremely likeable young man – this made it so much easier for us. Straight after this visit I made contact with Joy of Parents' Friend who gave us a lot of encouragement and was generally supportive.

The last really big hurdle to date was telling Tom's rugby-playing brothers! As Tom couldn't visit them, he wrote both a letter and we took it to them on two separate weekends. We spent a lot of time worrying about their reaction, but apart from being stunned, they said it made no difference to their relationship with Tom. They both wrote and told him this and offered their support.

As I write, it's nearly a year since the 'gay news', and though far from being 'home and dry' our world has not collapsed, we have laughed and been happy, and we are growing in understanding all the time, thanks to knowing we have a gay son. I'd just like to share the words of Virginia Satir; they have helped us tremendously and I hope they will help others 'new' to the situation. 'Life is not the way it's supposed to be. It's the way it is. The way you cope with it is what makes the difference.'

Jackie

Suicide

Suicide is the leading cause of death among gay male, lesbian, bisexual and transsexual youth. They are part of two populations at serious risk of suicide; sexual minorities and the young.
> *Paul Gibson, LCSW therapist and*
> *program consultant, San Francisco*

In research carried out by Bell and Weinberg* it was found that twenty-five per cent of lesbians and twenty per cent of gay men had actually attempted suicide. Gay males were six times more likely to attempt it than heterosexual males. Lesbians were more than twice as likely to try than heterosexual women in the study. A majority of suicide attempts by homosexuals took place at the age of twenty or younger and nearly a third were before the age of seventeen.

At least five thousand young people now take their own lives each year; a high proportion of these suicides must be gay or lesbian. There are around 500,000 suicide attempts made by young people annually. Research shows that lesbian and gay youth are two to three times more likely to attempt suicide than straight youth, and it is thought that up to thirty per cent of actual suicides may be of non-heterosexual youth. Statistics from Minneapolis, Los Angeles and San Francisco show that more than fifty per cent of gay youth experience suicidal feelings, and serious depression.

Considering the way lesbians, gay and bisexual young people

* *Homosexuality: A Study of Diversity Among Men and Women,* New York: Simon and Schuster, 1978

are treated once they are out to family, it is not surprising how many are at high risk of suicide. In an American study in 1985, Ramafedi found that half the young gay males he studied had experienced negative parental response to their sexuality; twenty-six per cent were forced to leave home for this reason.

It is gratifying that most parents ringing the Parents' Friend helpline actually wish to understand and support the children who have come out to them. Unfortunately, we are also well aware that those who would turn out their lesbian, gay or bisexual offspring once they knew of their sexuality, are the ones who would not consider ringing a helpline for support. Parents who come to our support group meetings have had to deal regularly with suicide attempts, sometimes more than once.

When there are few good role models for non-heterosexual youth to follow, except for the camp comedy acts on TV, where do young lesbians, gays and bisexuals turn for guidance? Unless they search out other non-heterosexuals who feel good about themselves and who can give them the confidence and self-esteem they need, then the future is bleak, to say the least. Local lesbian, gay and bisexual switchboards and even youth groups can be the lifeline that keeps them sane. Otherwise, it is uncertain what a less than confident young person can do, with little self-esteem and no prospect of finding acceptance either at home or in society at large.

Approximately two years ago my youngest son told my husband and myself, in a letter, that he was gay. We were devastated. We had no idea and it came as a complete shock. It didn't alter our feelings for our son and in no way did we feel like abandoning him. We were just terribly upset. I immediately phoned to tell him, through my tears, that I still loved him and would always be there for him.

Last year I came across a leaflet which our son had sent to us – it was from Parents' Friend. I rang the number and had a long and tearful talk. Talking to someone else who has gone through a similar experience makes you feel less alone. We can now talk to our son about his homosexuality and even make jokes about it.

I suppose it is a little easier for us because our son lives in another town. The only others who know are his two older brothers. He told them a year ago and they accepted it very well – far better, in fact, than I thought they would. The reason I can't tell the rest of the family and friends about our son, I think, is because I cannot bear anyone to think badly of him.

Our son has since told us that at one time he felt suicidal and went to the doctor for help. The thing that upset me most was that I didn't know and wasn't there for him. I'm so thankful he didn't do this dreadful thing and now knows he can come to us for help, no matter what.

Dorothy

The lack of self-worth non-heterosexuals feel as a consequence of societal rejection often results in absolute isolation; many parents who attend Parents' Friend meetings worry about their children's lack of social skills and constant habit of shutting themselves in their rooms, never speaking to a soul and refusing food, including the sharing of family meals. It is important to watch for such signs of withdrawal, and to have support available.

Although lesbian, gay and bisexual offspring may hate themselves in the beginning for being different, they will usually realize their self-worth eventually, perhaps with the help of their non-heterosexual and often heterosexual friends. In struggling to make the gay feelings go away, many learn to deal with their anger and frustration at being different, and find great strength in this. If our lesbian, gay and bisexual daughters and sons are helped to accept their difference at a very early age, they will be able to value themselves as we all should be able to do, regardless of our sexuality.

Let us look towards a future when we are all accepted as equal members of the human race, when suicide due to sexuality is no longer a statistic to be used in a book of this nature.

Groups, Helplines and Contacts

'Come to the edge,' he said.
They said 'We are afraid.'
'Come to the edge,' he said.
They came.
He pushed them,
and they flew. . . .
     Guillaume Apollinaire

The importance of contacts, groups and helplines cannot be overestimated. The Parents' Friend helpline was opened in 1987 and our first group meeting was on St Valentine's Day 1988. When we founded Parents' Friend, there were parents already acting as contacts.

It was 1969 – one year after the law legalizing homosexual acts in private. I had discovered that my third son was gay and was surprised and bewildered. By chance I switched on Woman's Hour on the Radio and heard a lady called Rose talking about a similar problem. I wrote to her via the BBC and we corresponded for a time. She was setting up a team to counsel other parents like ourselves – would I help?

In my ignorance I agreed, little realizing my lack of knowledge of the subject. I soon had to learn by ferreting books from libraries and purchasing the sparse literature available in those early years.

Sometimes I was overwhelmed by the sheer magnitude of the different problems encountered – wives, mothers, husbands, children, neighbours, workmates and so on – all with heartbreak and bewilderment. My task over the past twenty-four years has been to just listen, send out literature and lend books.

The organization that started then was called Parents'

Enquiry, one of the first self-help groups of any subject formed in England.

When my husband died, twelve years ago, I confirmed that my fourth child, my daughter, was lesbian. This was equally hard to adjust to, with more reading up of a different subject, and trying to gain knowledge of her culture which is not the same as my son's.

To add to my experiences, I then met and fell in love with a vicar. After about a year it slowly dawned on me that he was gay! Another blow, but I soon knew the heartache of wives of gay husbands and can relate with understanding.

Over the years, much has changed. With the onset of HIV/ AIDS in 1981, just when a little tolerance was creeping in, the virus plunged parents into deeper worries.

I have found it easier to talk on radio or TV, than to listen to an agonized parent over the phone. It is hard to hear a father sobbing or a mother's trembling voice and even much anger, on the phone. That's why I feel the anonymity of a helpline is invaluable.

Sometimes, after an hour or so, parents will say they feel clearer in mind just by talking it out. It has been gratifying recently to learn of the other various help groups which are now active, some started by parents I counselled in the past, and it is with great joy that I see these groups now uniting.

Norah

Rose and **Arthur** act as contacts in Shrewsbury, and the way they started a helpline was rather unusual:

About eight years ago the London Lesbian and Gay Centre at Cowcross Street, in its first year (GLC funded – just) put on an open day for parents and friends. Geoff, Arthur's son by a previous marriage, invited us along, as we were staying over that weekend with him in London. Geoff was on the Management Committee.

At this open day we met several other parents and it was suggested that parents needed their own counselling and support. We offered to do a newsletter, if any parent would subscribe £1 for paper and postage (things seemed much cheaper then!). In

*order to test the need and get a postal list, we wrote an open
letter to parents and Geoff eventually had it duplicated. Piles of
letters were left at various gay venues, including Cowcross Street
Centre. In short, we had no takers.*

*Geoff was rather vague as to why, but we gathered it was be-
cause gays seem to tell parents last, if at all, and thus were not
using the letter. Geoff was in a great proselytizing phase and
pushed us to do something special for parents. He gave us the
name and telephone number of a parents' group, and its meeting
times. After a brief correspondence we met the group's founders,
and they suggested a phoneline approach.*

*Around that time, Gay Switchboard stabilized its 'home' in
Shrewsbury and we paid for its first year's rental and said they
could put any parent in contact with us direct by phone or via
letter, c/o Switchboard's box number.*

*We had only one parent contact us via Switchboard, but not
only were we able to support her, our relationship has developed
into friendship for over five years now. This is one of the great
things about parents' groups – often, good friendships are made.*

*Initially, though, contacts are often distraught, weepy and angry.
Some come across on the phone as self-righteous bigots who need
very careful handling to prevent our being discredited as a counselling service (even though it's free, with unpaid volunteers, the
standard of ethics must be very high and awareness of law, cul-
tural mores and their pitfalls is necessary).*

*Recently, Arthur has been on a couple of local radio talk-ins
around gay issues but we've never had parents contact us from
these programmes. Because we travel a lot, and thus are often
away from the home phone, we have not furthered publicity ourselves.
There are few parents in our immediate area with whom we could
form a group and pass on the role of main contact. This saddens
us, but is generally true of many minority groups in rural areas.*

Other groups were set up around the same time as Parents'
Friend. Leicester Parents' Group was one of these.

*I learned of my son's homosexuality about a year before the no-
torious Clause 28 was conceived. It become law in May 1988, as
Section 28 of the Local Government Act, and stated that local*

councils should not 'promote' homosexuality. This word has not, to this day, ever been fully explained, but in its unexplained meaning it can lead to such a lot of discrimination against our children.

The increased publicity and media discussion about Clause 28 gave rise to new and powerful emotions. TV discussions and newspaper articles and letters included suggestions that 'they' should be sent to the gas chambers, isolated on islands, etc., etc. The fear of AIDS has strongly fuelled the public's prejudice.

All this time, I felt a lot of fear on behalf of our children and tremendous anger against the bigots who were creating this situation – the politicians.

At this time also, I had picked up a gay newspaper and noticed a short article about a group in Manchester and how they were fighting against that terrible clause. It was then I decided I had to start a group in Leicester.

I first spoke to a woman who had counselled gay people and their parents for twenty years. She was most encouraging and supportive. Then I contacted the local gay line and found the young man on the end of the line a great help. I will always be so grateful to him.

Finally, we got it together and, two years later, we were increasing our membership, making inroads into other institutions in the community, getting to know more people and organizations country-wide and even extending into Europe with personal contacts already in Holland.

The parents' group was very supportive of its members and the out members of our local gay community appreciated our existence and contribution.

Our wider involvement with the gay community greatly enriched us as individuals. We were certain that we, as parents, could make a positive contribution in working towards our children's equal rights in society.

Now, some years on, we are still battling away. The atmosphere has eased, somewhat, in that gay issues are seen and discussed far more frequently in the media, although the law still denies equality and basic civil rights to gays. On a personal level, I have gained in confidence and can talk about gay issues far more openly. I continue to be impressed at the strength that our parents' group has given its members.

It is such a pleasure to meet young gay people. It is such a tragedy that many of them live in fear of their parents' reactions to finding out about their sexuality.

If we can achieve some reduction in the number of personal miseries suffered and if we can teach some of the next generation that homosexuality is just a part of nature's complicated tapestry of life and if we can influence changes for the better in our laws regarding homosexuality, then the parents' group will have served its purpose.

Frances

*

On finding we had a gay son we never questioned this fact, our son not being one for exaggeration, simply one for plain facts.

I did, however, spend weeks waiting for the actual shock to set in and I rang every helpline I could find which dealt with gay issues. I have no idea how I knew there was a gay switchboard in Leeds, but I did and I rang, only to find Lesbian Line in operation that night. They were really helpful and put me in touch with other numbers and eventually I found other mothers who took calls from those who find themselves with non-heterosexual offspring. They were in London and I really wanted to meet others to whom this had happened and with whom I could talk.

One day a gay friend rang to say he was attending a meeting of a group to which he belonged and he thought Alan and I might like to meet the speaker. He said he'd try to arrange this with the secretary. He duly came back to us, asking which school our sons had attended, having realized that the secretary had taught both our sons and was a little worried that maybe we might blame him for our son's sexuality! I knew immediately which teacher this was, as I'd known he was gay for a long time and it had never bothered me as long as his teaching was faultless, which it was.

We met up with the speaker. I asked who she was and she said simply 'A mother with a gay son'. We chatted for a while and it turned out that she and two other mothers with lesbian and gay children had set up a parents' group. We were invited to their next meeting and she also said that, perhaps in the future, I might like to take calls in our area, just as the mothers in London had done earlier. I said this was not possible as I knew nothing about homosexuality whatsoever.

Since that day, we have done many things. Perhaps most importantly, towards the end of 1987 and in early 1988 we got involved with the fight against the notorious Clause 28, now Section 28 of the Local Government Act. The clause states that local councils must not 'promote' homosexuality. To this day, no one has been able to explain exactly what 'promote' means but this dreadful act has certainly affected our children who just happen to be lesbian, gay or bisexual, in a detrimental way.

I eventually decided to use our home telephone as a helpline for other parents finding they had non-heterosexual offspring. Soon I realized callers were asking to meet others like themselves, and the support group was set up. We never wished to give time to anything other than the helpline, but we have met every month since then and numerous mothers and fathers have attended, not to mention husbands and wives who have found themselves to be partners or spouses of lesbian, gay or bisexual people.

We called the helpline and group Parents' Friend, since Friend Gay Counselling in Bradford offered us the use of their address when we found the one we had paid for at the Post Office was not confidential. We aimed to ensure that our private life was kept apart from our Parents' Friend work.

I have always worked under a pseudonym as I felt my son had a right to privacy. I also found it much easier, as did other members of the family, to know instantly that a call on the private line was a Parents' Friend call and not someone who might be part of my personal life. Others in the family knew not to ask who was calling.

Before I began the helpline I asked my son if it was all right with him. He said it was, just as long as he was not expected to have any involvement whatsoever. We agreed and have never asked him to do anything for Parents' Friend. Our meeting venue has always been kept confidential and our members appreciate knowing for sure that no one without some involvement with a lesbian, gay or bisexual loved one would ever attend such a meeting.

We were very lucky, after Clause 28, to see advertised that one of the campaigning organizations had some money left over and that those needing funds for groups should get in touch. We *applied for funding for a dedicated telephone line or an answering machine and were given sufficient funds for both. This was a real help as we were then able to keep our personal lives and our volunteer work quite separate. It made a great deal of difference to family life.*

When I realized just how busy I was becoming with calls, I knew that I could not continue alone forever. Eventually, I met another mother locally (as some come from long distances) and we got on very well. I felt she would be an asset to us if she would agree to help. One day I found myself asking her, quite out of the blue, if she would help us with the line and the group. Just as I had done, she said she knew nothing. I explained that experience is the best teacher and I also knew that she had already gone out and learned a lot, and had even marched, locally, against the infamous Clause 28. I knew I had an ally and from that day Val has been part of the team and we work extremely well as three totally different individuals. We think very much alike and are all equally determined to see that our children achieve equality with all others. One way to do this is to educate and support their parents.

We are all extremely busy as we not only answer the helpline and run the group, but we produce a quarterly newsletter and speak to groups, gay, bisexual or otherwise. We are called upon to advise on articles for newspapers and magazines and are regularly invited to take part in radio discussions, phone-ins and television. Alan and I do not appear on television, since our son chooses not to tell the world of his sexuality (believing it is no one's business but his own or that of those he chooses to tell) and we would be coming out for him if we did so. Val takes on this task when possible.

We are in constant touch with other local and distant groups on gay issues and are told we give a good and much needed service to the community. We network with all other parents' groups throughout the country and we all work together where there is discrimination against gay people and when the feeling is that intervention by parents might help. We go by what lesbian, gay and bisexual people themselves tell us and they indicate when they feel we might be of assistance in helping a person or persons to understand the harm discrimination can cause.

In 1993 all the parents' groups with which we have regularly been in contact formed the political campaigning organization FFLAG (Families and Friends of Lesbians and Gays) and, in this way, parents' groups hope to have more strength in fighting discrimination, though as a registered charity, Parents' Friend itself cannot campaign politically.

We parents who support our non-heterosexual offspring can come in for a lot of abuse and the same prejudice and discrimination to which our children seem forever likely to be subjected, in spite of increasing public discussion. We can be seen as 'cranks' by some people who have been known to say that we are 'encouraging' our children to be gay. Those who say such things tend to be those who consider our children perverts and deviants, in choosing their sexuality. This is utter nonsense. The only choice our children have is to accept their sexuality and feel good about it, or to suppress it.

Alan and I are so glad we set up Parents' Friend, but Val shares our wish that we could be made redundant tomorrow through society's acceptance of our children. Until that wonderful day in the not-too-far-distant future, we hope, we will continue to work with parents, husbands and wives and look forward to the world becoming a far better place. Until parents can accept their non-heterosexual offspring totally, what hope is there for others to do so? We will continue to struggle with society generally. Open mindedness and free-thinking are what we look to, and we hope that this anthology will help towards this.

Joy and Alan, founders
of Parents' Friend

If we can help you to understand and accept your daughter's or son's sexuality we will do so. We each have different experiences of our own child coming out. We all deal with it in our own way. We all come through to the other end feeling far better people for having had the experience. And we all feel privileged to have one or more lesbian, gay or bisexual members of our family.

Our understanding of our children is encapsulated in the words of the poet and philosopher Kahlil Gibran:

Your children are not your children.
They are the sons and daughters of Life's longing for itself.
They come through you but not from you,
And though they are with you yet they belong not to you.

You may give them your love but not your thoughts,
For they have their own thoughts.
You may house their bodies but not their souls,
For their souls dwell in the house of tomorrow,
which you cannot visit, not even in your dreams.
You may strive to be like them, but seek
not to make them like you.

At Parents' Friend we simply say: 'We love our lesbian, gay
and bisexual children.'

PASTELS

Storms make oaks take deeper root.

George Herbert

Why do lesbians, gays and bisexuals marry? That is a question asked often on the PASTELS (Partners' And Spouses' Telephone Support) Helpline, by parents, husbands, wives and partners. There are numerous answers to this question but the most common is *to make it go away*. Non-heterosexuals often hate themselves and feel they do not fit anywhere. They feel like the only person on earth who is attracted to the same gender. They are confused, and they see others getting on with their lives, in relationships with those of the opposite gender.

Lesbian and gay children grow up to know they must conform to this kind of behaviour when they do not feel comfortable with close friends of the opposite gender. They may even think that all young people feel like they do, but for some peculiar reason act in quite the opposite way. The confusion remains with them throughout their early life, continues into adolescence and naïvely into adulthood. Some will understand what it is all about but, knowing society's attitude, they may push it deep inside their very being; unfortunately, this is only a temporary solution, and the feelings are bound to surface at some point in their marriage. This may be a week into the marriage, as was the case with one couple. The wife rang our helpline in the middle of packing her belongings to leave her new husband before he returned from work. They had lived together for a number of years, and only after marriage did he decide to come out to her. That 'bit of paper' made it all too final for the husband who had gone ahead with the marriage because he felt it was what she had wanted, and also 'to make it go away'; he realized it simply was not going to do that. He was gay and that was an end to it. The wife was devastated, but she also feared for his mental state. It certainly does not go away, even after twenty or thirty years in a marriage where one partner is living a permanent lie.

Calls to the helpline come regularly from heterosexuals with a great number of years invested in a relationship with a lesbian, gay or bisexual partner, and the heterosexual partner has had no idea whatsoever. There may be married children, and even grandchildren, yet their partner's different sexuality has not gone away with the marriage and has suddenly become an issue to be considered. The trigger for each person is different. Maybe they have bottled their feelings up for so long that they will have a breakdown if they don't tell someone. They may have gone into counselling to sort out some other problem in their life and found that their sexuality became topmost on the agenda. Others have, for the first time, met someone who brings out those deeply hidden feelings and there is no longer any way of denying the true facts. Up to this point the individual may never have engaged in sexual activity with a person of the same gender.

In some instances the heterosexual will notice a change in their partner but be unable to put a finger on the reasons, even after much discussion between the two of them. The marriage may not have been successful sexually but the rest of the relationship has been wonderful, and someone who has had no previous experience with anyone of the same gender will think either they are somehow at fault, or that this is how it is for all couples in spite of what TV and the papers tell us.

Some heterosexual partners who ring the helpline say that they have always blamed themselves for the unsatisfactory sexual side of the marriage, and now they realize it was not them, even though their partner has led them to feel responsible. Many feel relieved, but wonder if they have never meant anything to their partner, or if they were used to make it right for their loved one. In our experience at Parents' Friend, we have realized that the love the couple shared when they seemed to be in a really good relationship, is usually real and honest love and their partners confirm this. Sadly, this is not so for others, who felt for a long time that there was something lacking, but it was elusive. When the pieces fit together and the anger has subsided, most heterosexual callers are unbelievably reasonable, wanting nothing but to understand and support their partner. I can only admire these men and women.

When the marriage does not feel right for either partner, the stress will affect both of them. If sensible, they will sit down to talk over the situation. The non-heterosexual partner will fight against coming out, avoiding the inevitable split. There will be so much stress around the two that every little thing that goes wrong will bring about arguments. Life together will become unbearable. Relate may seem to be the only answer; some find a lot of help there, others are not so fortunate, as it all depends on the counsellor allocated to them. For some it will bring about the disclosure, for others, things remain as they were.

Married gay men, once out to their wives, usually declare a wish to remain together. They will sometimes also expect their wife to agree to their frequenting gay clubs, bringing gay friends home, going on holiday with gay friends, but, to all intents and purposes, maintaining the appearance of an ordinary heterosexual marriage to the outside world.

Some will expect their wives to leave home, with the children. These findings come from our experience in listening to callers to the helpline, and not from sheer fantasy on my part. However, many married gay men feel very guilty and responsible for having brought misery to their wives and families.

Our research has shown that women who come out to their husbands will most often leave the marriage home, usually with the children, sometimes not; their husbands, though terribly upset, and often angry at first, may be very understanding once they have discussed the situation at length. They usually wish their wife to remain with them, although most lesbians will move out on finding a partner and beginning another relationship. If the lesbian relationship has existed for some time before the wife comes out to her husband, then she will most likely move out fairly soon.

In the case of both men and women coming out to their partners, there is every chance that they will continue to be the very best of friends. Some will remain in the marriage, but live separate lives quite happily. Others will attempt to make the marriage work in spite of everything else, especially when there are young children. This is not usually successful, and there will be a split later. Some couples will live together quite amicably for the rest of their lives. There will always, it seems, be heterosexual fathers who go to court for custody of their children, insisting that their wife, now lesbian, is not a good mother and role model for her children. And there will always be wives who go to court insisting that their gay or bisexual husbands are a threat to their children now they are out. Those husbands have not changed in any way and will be no less able to treat their children well on visits or to take them on outings now than before coming out.

Children brought up in a lesbian or gay household, or with one lesbian, gay or bisexual parent will understand much more about alternative ways of living and be more accepting of difference. In no way will homosexuality 'rub off' on any child and it is a fact that most non-heterosexuals have heterosexual parents – not all, but most. No one can *make* another person gay. (One mother ringing the helpline expressed a wish to knock her daughter's head on a wall until her gayness was forced out of her; but even she knew this was, unfortunately for her, impossible.)

I fell in love three years ago with a really wonderful man who is very sensitive and very kind. However, he is homosexual. He knows how I feel and has been incredibly understanding and, of course, I do realize we can have no future together. It has taken me a long time and a lot of heartache to come to the point where I can see the whole thing logically.

We see a lot of one another as we both enjoy similar pastimes. I would like to turn my love into friendship – not easy. I believe and hope I may be able to do this and hope he will feel he can do the same.

Although I would have said I am not prejudiced, I have realized I had the belief that gays chose to be that way and, therefore, by implication, could choose not to be. James has made me realize this is not so but that something in his nature makes him the way he is. I think, in some ways, he would rather conform to the 'norm' but simply cannot do this.

I think a lot of people share my earlier misconception. However, I recognize that there is still a lot I don't understand, and know I am not alone in this.

Elaine

*

I had been married for twenty-three years when I found out that my husband was gay. It is hard to describe the devastating effect this had on me.

I went through every conceivable emotion. At first I was relieved to know what had been causing the problems in our marriage and was full of sympathy for the painful conflict my husband had been going through. Then came the pain of anger, resentment, betrayal and loss. I felt so helpless, so alone, with a problem I couldn't discuss with anyone and that had no visible solution.

There were times when I felt it was all my fault. How could I have lived with him for twenty-three years and yet not really known him at all? Many times I felt desperate and suicidal. It was only the thought of what such an action would do to my husband and two teenage children that stopped me.

I searched frantically for help and was amazed to find how little existed for a woman in my position. I found every kind of support group for gay people but nothing for wives, despite being told that there are thousands of women going through this pain. Then I made contact with Parents' Friend and they told me about their offshoot, PASTELS. They gave me contact numbers and, at last, I was able to speak to other women who really knew what I was going through.

My husband and I have separated now but we are the very best of friends. In many ways our relationship is better now than it has ever been. We still love each other and enjoy recalling the happy times we have spent together.

It would be all too easy to feel I had wasted twenty-three years but, of course, I haven't. We have two wonderful children who have been of so much support to both my husband and myself, and at forty-two there is still a lot more life to live and I intend to enjoy it.

> *It is true, my life has changed dramatically. I have lost my husband, but I have gained the* very best friend *anyone could wish for.*
>
> *Fiona*

Fiona is now a PASTELS contact.

The problem of telling the children is little different to that of parents telling their children of the gayness of a sibling, but it can be extremely upsetting for the children to find Mummy or Daddy is not heterosexual. They can be left with the nasty comments made by friends, relations or neighbours. Eventually they learn to deal with it, but it can never be plain sailing for anyone in this position. By the time teenage children are told, they may easily have taken on prejudiced feelings for anything other than the 'norm'. They should be encouraged to look further into the subject and see if they really believe all the bad things they have heard about people like their parent, who was fine until she or he came out. There are books to help in this and the P.F. *Guide for Parents Who Have Lesbian, Gay or Bisexual Children* is not only a good resource for parents, but for anyone who wishes to understand better how some people just happen not to be heterosexual.

The best support anyone can ever have is from others who have had a similar experience and know the feelings they had at the time. The PASTELS helpline is really a referral point, where callers may offload their upset feelings and are then given contact telephone numbers of others who have 'been there'. At the time of writing, we have far more women contacts than men and would consider any man who has found himself married to, or the partner of, a lesbian or bisexual woman, as a contact for the PASTELS helpline.

The Church – Religious Beliefs and Attitudes

> Rather light a candle than complain about the darkness.
>
> *Chinese proverb*

Parents who consider themselves to be good Christians and find their daughter or son is not heterosexual may either say 'love conquers all', and feel that nothing could ever come between them and their love for their child, or they may find themselves struggling with 'what the Bible says' (or what they think the Bible says) about homosexuality. Many Christians regularly cite Biblical support for their condemnation of homosexuality, but cannot cite specific texts as 'proof'. They may also repeat 'God said' or 'Jesus said', without clarifying exactly *what* they said.

In fact, Jesus said *nothing* about homosexuality. What God is supposed to have said came from other sources. The Bible does not give guidance of any sort to those with same-sex orientation to life or homosexual love. It does, however, give specific guidance on other subjects, and today that guidance is considered outmoded or irrelevant by the same people who condemn homosexuality. For instance, the food laws in Leviticus 11.1–8 are now disregarded by most Christians, as are the injunctions against long hair (1 Corinthians 11.14) and women teachers (1 Timothy 2.11–12). It is quite clear that no one takes any notice of all this nowadays; why do anti-gay Christians make rash statements based on complex interpretative issues and obsolete customs? Most of the Bible can be read very differently today than it was when first written.

The story of Sodom, from the book of Genesis, is a case in

point. It tells of two angels who visited the city of Sodom, where a man named Lot invited them to stay with him overnight. The angels accepted and Lot provided food and shelter for them. As they were about to take to their beds, a crowd of men came to the house and demanded that the visitors be taken outside so 'that we may know them'. Lot asked that the visitors be allowed to rest in preparation for their journey in the morning. He begged the crowd not to force themselves on his visitors and offered them instead his two (virgin) daughters 'who have not known men': 'do to them as you please'. The crowd was unappeased, and Lot's visitors pulled him inside his home for safety.

In the Old Testament, the Hebrew word *yadha* (as in Genesis 19.5) meant 'to know', as in 'to identify a person'. But another interpretation – 'to have sexual intercourse with' (as in Genesis 19.7) is clearly the sense of Lot's offer of his daughters to the crowd of men. That Lot should offer his virgin daughters to men intent on violence seems far less unacceptable to some Christians than that the villagers should 'know' the visiting angels.

However, there is another way of understanding this text. Some Christians believe that the villagers came to Lot's house to inspect his visitors' credentials – or in other words, to *identify* them. Lot, as a newcomer to Sodom, would not have been allowed to entertain visitors without establishing their identity first. He would have been aware of this, but would also have felt that his visitors might be upset if he allowed them, as very special guests, to be harrassed by the men of the city. So the 'Sin of Sodom' can be interpreted as one of inhospitality, rather than homosexuality. Another text (Luke 10.1–15) seems to echo this idea. There, Jesus stated that his disciples would be sent forth to spread the gospel; if they visited a town that refused to receive them, they were not to linger but to advise the inhabitants that the Kingdom of God was near: 'it shall be more tolerable in that day for Sodom, than for that city'. There is, therefore, some doubt as to whether the Bible refers to sexual intercourse or to hospitality in the story of Sodom, and it is impossible to say for certain that the city was destroyed because of homosexuality (sodomy).

From the New Testament, 1 Corinthians 6.9–10 is quoted

against homosexuality. As there are several possible transla-
tions of the Greek words *malakoi* and *arsenokoitoi* (*arsenokoitoi*
also appears in 1 Timothy 1.9–10), no one can actually insist
on an undisputed meaning. The problem with attempting to
apply the language of the Bible to modern-day situations is
that interpretation conflicts.

Some parents, like **Roberta**, may still find comfort in the
Bible or in their religion:

> *My son was 19 when it all came out in the open. I am a single*
> *parent and even though it almost broke my heart I was so relieved*
> *to have it out at last. I went (unknown to my son) everywhere I*
> *could think of for help, but finally found consolation in the Bible.*

> *

> *It is hard to explain to some people that it is not a problem hav-*
> *ing a lesbian daughter. The problem does not lie with us but*
> *with the people who make it a problem. The real evil is with the*
> *religious fanatics who use religion to make homosexuality a 'sin'.*
> *The one thing they seem to forget is that the God whom they*
> *believe created all things also created our sons and daughters as*
> *they are. . . .*

> *Angela*

Andrea, like Roberta, finds consolation in her faith:

> *Our son told us he was gay after his first term at university. It*
> *was a tremendous shock. I think my husband and I were numb*
> *because it was so completely unexpected and a totally new experi-*
> *ence. We didn't know any gays, or so we thought. The thing that*
> *helped us was our son's very sensible statement. 'I'm still the*
> *same person I was five minutes ago before I told you' – and this*
> *was perfectly true.*
>
> *I am a Quaker, a member of the Religious Society of Friends,*
> *and knew there was much Quaker writing about sexuality that*
> *we had not felt it necessary to read. Now we did and were greatly*
> *helped by it. In the Foreword to one book it says: 'The Quaker*
> *way has always been to approach life experimentally and*

undogmatically, not to judge by predetermined standards but to respect the many forms in which "that of God in every one" may be revealed.'

Most Friends (Quakers) are very open and accepting and we soon found that we came to know and form close friendships with a number of gay people, many of whom we found to be unusually sensitive and perceptive.

*

I was interested that the Parents' Friend booklet quotes that wonderful passage from Paul (1 Corinthians 13). If you go back to 1 Corinthians 6 you find a rather different Paul. I read it in a Bible I came upon by accident and was quite shocked, perhaps because it is put into modern English. In the old King James Version the word 'effeminate' is used, but in The Living Bible it says: 'Those who live immoral lives – who are idol worshippers, adulterers or homosexuals – will have no share in His Kingdom.'

No wonder there are problems when a modern version of the Bible puts it so crudely. I have always thought that the Bible was a rather dangerous book; it can almost be made to mean anything that you want it to. It seems that putting it into modern language does not help very much. I do often wonder, however, whether my son ever read this passage and was shocked by it. He was not a church-goer but this was his Bible.

Paula

At Parents' Friend we concur with Goethe: 'Our differences are God's gift to the world.'

Our colleague on the Parents' Friend/PASTELS helpline in Leeds had to look carefully at what some good Christians really think about homosexual people.

One cold November Sunday evening I was at home with my 18-year-old foster son, Paul, who had drunk two bottles of red wine. He suddenly became upset and said 'I've got AIDS.'

He hadn't been well for some time and at that time there was a lot on TV and in the papers about AIDS and he had previously asked me if I thought this was what was wrong with him. As he had told me he had never had sex I couldn't see how he would have AIDS.

I asked him how he could have AIDS if he hadn't had sex. He then started to cry and said 'I'm a poof and a queer.' I told him not to call himself those names and asked if he was telling me he was gay. I tried to comfort him but he kept pushing me away. I told him it made no difference, I still loved him and we would set about educating ourselves, neither of us knowing much about homosexuality.

That night I didn't sleep at all. Even though I had suspected since he was sixteen that he might be gay, it was still a shock to be told. I felt as if I'd been kicked in the stomach.

Luckily I had never had any feelings against homosexuals so there was no problem in accepting it – it was just another thing in life to learn more about.

For a number of weeks I had very mixed-up feelings. In spite of the fact I'd suspected Paul might be gay it still hadn't oc-curred to me that this was what was worrying him so much. I felt betrayed that he had lied to me when we were so close. I started looking at all men and wondering if they too were gay and could I really trust anyone?

He asked me not to tell anyone – not even my husband, as he thought he would turn him out.

The next three weeks were a nightmare whilst we waited for the results of the HIV test Paul had decided on. This was the only way he would be convinced he didn't have the HIV virus, even though I knew, if what he had told me was true, he could not possibly be HIV positive. I was, however, just as worried as he was.

I went along to the STD clinic with him. After what seemed an eternity we finally received the results, which were negative. Paul's health improved after this. The worry had obviously brought on his illness.

We then decided to set about educating ourselves on homosexu-ality. We talked a lot and read whatever we could find on the subject. We watched anything relevant on TV. There seemed to be quite a lot on TV at that time but I suppose this was really us noticing everything touching on the subject and perhaps there wasn't any more than there had ever been – it just felt there was.

After a year of keeping it to ourselves Paul decided to come out as he was fed up with leading a double life.

We all attended the local church to worship and socialize. This is where I met my foster son who had gone there since he was

*ten. He was really well liked. For a few years he had been a server
in the church and had just been appointed by the Bishop of Ripon
to administer the chalice. When he came out, people were stunned
but said it was all right; then after a month everything blew up.
One or two people refused to take Communion from him and
walked out of church. At a committee meeting a lot of terrible
things were said to his face and to my husband also. I was told
that because I accepted Paul I was encouraging him. At one point
it was said that Paul could take Communion but it would have
to be after everyone else in case he passed on AIDS! Paul couldn't
face any more and decided to leave the church, which we all did
as a family. The committee meeting ended with my son and the
vicar in tears in each other's arms. The clergy, I have to say,
were extremely supportive right the way through.*

*The church had been the one thing that meant so much in his
life, particularly after his mother's death from cancer. I simply
could not accept how people called themselves Christians and yet
could treat someone in this way. I had always believed in a God
of love but the things that were said to us certainly did not confirm this in any way. Although we began to attend another church,
my heart wasn't in it. I still believe in God but very rarely go to
church now, as I find it hard to accept how hypocritical the church
and its people – the so-called Christians – can be.*

*It has taken years for the feelings of rejection to pass. Even now I
really don't trust people. Paul doesn't go to church at all now and
those loving and caring Christian people will never know just how
they tore Paul apart. They will never have any idea of what they
took away from him at a time in his life when he needed the support
of friends and the church more than at any other time.*

*When we told our other three children, two of them took it all
right, although they were surprised as they hadn't guessed about
Paul being gay. Our married son reacted very badly and told us
to turn Paul out or we would not be allowed to see our granddaughter. My daughter-in-law was fine though. My little
granddaughter couldn't understand why Daddy seemed to hate
Paul when she had always adored him. After hours of talking,
my married son finally agreed it wouldn't be fair to deprive his
daughter of her grandparents' love and contact. He also allowed
her to meet Paul although for years he himself didn't speak to*

Paul and there was a dreadful atmosphere when they were both in the house together. Paul was not allowed to visit their home and this upset our granddaughter a lot. She once said 'No matter what Daddy thinks of Paul I will always love him.' When she was ten years old I explained everything to her as she kept asking me why we had left the church and why Daddy didn't like Paul. Also, Paul read her the book Jenny Lives with Eric and Martin *which she understood perfectly well. She now sticks up amazingly for gay people if she hears nasty things being said, especially in school.*

I am glad Paul had the courage to be himself and come out. When people ask me if he has a girlfriend I just say he is gay. Some of his boyfriends I like, others I don't. It would be the same if he was heterosexual and had girlfriends.

I often wonder why God chose to send him into my life but I am so glad he did.

Val

Dub, in America, has already described his son's coming out and likened it to 'The Big Bang'. He now relates how his attitudes towards organized religion, and those of his wife, Joyce, underwent great change after his son came out. He also describes how the evangelical right of the local Christian churches caused other problems, in which he and many others were involved:

In Dan Barker's book, Losing Faith in Faith, *the point is made that becoming a freethinker doesn't happen overnight. We ex-religious persons arrived at free thought by an educational process – long for some, short for others.*

Barker maintains that there is no magic bullet and no short stream of twenty-five words or less that converts a believer into a non-believer in one fell swoop. However some of us experience a 'magic moment'. It might be an event that serves as a catalyst to make all the ingredients of that ongoing educational process suddenly combine. In that moment we become 'born-again freethinkers'. . . .

Though neither Joyce, my wife, nor I expressed it verbally at the time, in retrospect both she and I agree we had experienced the 'magic moment' at precisely the same time, in the aftermath of events following the revelation of our son's being gay.

Except for Christmas and Easter, our family generally had abandoned religious observances and church by the time our children entered high school. The subject was rarely discussed. As I look back on it, each of us in his or her own way had already embarked on independent journeys in the direction of free thought.

Long before we knew our son was gay, both Joyce and I were educated enough to know that homosexuality is not a choice, but an innate trait, probably originating in the womb from a combination of genetic and hormonal factors. No one would willingly choose to be gay. But the discovery that a family member is gay or lesbian brings many people to a turn in the road, where a genuine choice may have to be made: the choice between what most religions and their scriptures have to say, and what recent scientific and medical evidence strongly supports. The decision that Joyce and I made to leave religion entirely turned on this one choice.

Before 1988 rolled around, Joyce and I had discovered the two organizations that have made such a difference in our lives. Dan Barker's appearances on several talk shows about that time prompted us to join the Freedom From Religion Foundation. During a visit to the library, Joyce learned of a nearby group affiliated with PFLAG – The National Federation of Parents and Friends of Lesbians and Gays.

PFLAG is made up largely of heterosexual parents, friends and families of homosexuals. Local PFLAG chapters provide support groups for those new to the situation of having a lesbian, gay or bisexual family member. Local chapters and the national headquarters in Washington, D.C., are involved in educational efforts through literature, talk shows and speakers' bureaux, and the Federation provides opportunities at all levels for parents to become advocates for the rights of their lesbian, gay or bisexual children.

PFLAG now (early 1993) has more than 300 chapters in the United States and 11 other countries. For over four years, Joyce has been a member of the National Board and serves as Southeast Regional Director, covering the Carolinas, Georgia, Tennessee, Florida and Puerto Rico. In each of these states and elsewhere, many parents, including ourselves, have willingly marched and participated in Gay Pride Rallies and other events. We have witnessed first-hand the bible-waving preachers and their minions harassing our kids. Fundamentalist preachers of every color have

assaulted us and our children with bull horns yelling the usual
blatherings of biblical hellfire and damnation.

Our first open encounter with the Religious Right occurred in
April 1989. We picketed Vice-President Dan Quayle in the spring
of 1989 when he made a speech to a local fundamentalist group,
'The Concerned Charlotteans', organized, they say, to promote
traditional family values. They spend most of their time promoting hatred for homosexuals and people who support gay rights.
The Concerned Charlotteans also devote energy to promoting prayer
in schools, to closing adult book stores, to censoring books in the
libraries and trying to ban abortion clinics, state lotteries and
alcohol sales. The head of this organization is a Church of God
preacher named Joe Chambers – friend of Jesse Helms.

At a banquet of the Concerned Charlotteans, Dan Quayle de-
voted his entire speech to his views on traditional families. Meanwhile, on the sidewalks outside the Civic Centre marched an
assortment of picketers. There were gays and lesbians, in addition to abortion rights activists and representatives of other libertarian causes. But what grabbed the media's attention were six
parents marching in support of our gay children with banners
stating 'I LOVE MY GAY SON' and 'THE BIGOTS ARE HAV-
ING QUAYLE FOR DINNER'.

In 1990, when President George Bush came to Charlotte to
stump for Jesse Helms's re-election, a larger number of parents
showed up to protest. Having become bolder and more activist,
Charlotte's PFLAG chapter became the first in the nation to have
picketed both the President and the Vice-President. We received a
smattering of national publicity, but nothing compared to 1991.

PFLAG holds annual conventions. The relatively small city of
Charlotte was selected to host the milestone Tenth Annual PFLAG
Convention in the fall of 1991. The Charlotte chapter designated
Joyce and me to co-chair the event.

The Religious Right mounted a vigorous campaign to try and
stop us. The Concerned Charlotteans spent thousands of dollars
to print newsletters and buy cable TV and radio time to spread
unbelievable distortions and outright lies about PFLAG. First they
attempted to strong-arm the hotel into cancelling our convention. The hotel stood its ground and became one of our staunchest
allies. Attempts were made to intimidate the Chamber of Com-

merce and the Convention Bureau. Those agencies also were supportive of PFLAG and ignored the 'funny mentalists'. (I know
they're 'funny', but I don't understand the 'mentalist' part.)

I would, however, be remiss if I failed to mention that our
convention was widely supported by mainstream churches, particularly the Episcopalean and Unitarians.

Joe Chambers became desperate. Leading newspaper editorials
assured the populace that 500 heterosexual parents from four countries would have no more effect on the city than an American
Legion Convention. Chambers predicted that Charlotte would be
inundated by thousands of homosexuals bent on sodomizing the
city's youngsters with the blessing and approval of their equally
depraved parents!

We discovered that someone had planted a mole on our mailing
list to receive all of our convention literature, resulting in our printed
materials reaching all-time highs of perverse sickness in their misin-
terpretation. Chambers appeared on a Christian TV 60-minute pro-
gramme and by the end it wasn't clear whether he had concluded
that all homosexuals are atheists or that all atheists are homosexuals!

One disturbed woman phoned the call-in show to tell Chambers
how frightened she was that Satan's demons would begin possessing
all the office buildings in downtown Charlotte (downtown being
the main business part of the city) near the hotel to contaminate
the city with AIDS. One man called to say that he thought all
good Christians should take their guns into the hotel and shoot
all the devils on sight. 'No, no, brother,' said Chambers, 'we must
show these people compassion and urge them to turn from their
sinful ways.' (And this was only the parents!)

Hotel security and the police cordoned off the hotel and downtown area more tightly than when Bush and Quayle came to town.
A major network flew in camera crew from New York City to
cover our convention.

The whole event was a big success for us and a big bust for
Ol' Joe. Usually Joe and The Concerned Charlotteans attract dozens
of volunteers but this time he mostly picketed alone or with one
or two others on the hotel sidewalk. His tactics had backfired. He
had even frightened away his most ardent supporters in the fundamentalist evangelical communities. Neither Joe nor the city of
Charlotte will ever be the same again!

HIV/AIDS

The only thing that frightens me when my son rings and tells me he feels tired, exhausted or he has flu, at the back of my mind is AIDS, even though he promises he practises safer sex and isn't promiscuous.

It would be remiss in a book of this nature to omit mention of HIV/AIDS, but we who work as parent contacts look on HIV/AIDS not simply as a gay issue but one for every person regardless of their sexuality. The media manipulated the publicity of HIV/AIDS to the extent that society in general was encouraged to believe the virus affected only gay or bisexual men. Common sense might have suggested that a virus does not home in on select categories of people.

AIDS is something that everyone should take account of, even if we are sexually active but in a monogamous long-term relationship. AIDS has been diagnosed in this country since around 1980, but in other countries for much longer, so one must ask oneself if care has always been taken during sex. Have you used safer sex methods such as condoms and has your partner (or partners) done the same? If you are a drug-user, have you always used sterile needles or works? Could they have been shared with someone who might be infected with the HIV virus? Some individuals have received infected blood or blood products before these began to be treated to kill the virus. An increasing number of babies are acquiring the disease via HIV-positive mothers. These are the main ways in which the HIV virus can be transmitted. The motto for sexually active people is 'LOVE SAFELY'.

Having said all this, AIDS does seem to affect gay men to a

greater extent in the western world, but in the world as a whole more heterosexuals are affected than homosexuals. Lesbians are thought to be in a low risk group according to 'behaviour'; this is the only way high or low risk people can be described in relation to the HIV virus. It is not what or who we are, but what we do that puts us into any risk group. There are no low or high risk groups relating to our sexuality. We can all act safely or unsafely.

What is AIDS?

AIDS is a condition in which the body's natural ability to fight off infections is broken down, leading to a number of life-threatening illnesses. The condition was first recognized in the early 1980s in America and is now recognized world-wide.

AIDS is caused by a virus called HIV (Human Immuno-deficiency Virus). The virus has the potential once inside the body to destroy certain types of white blood cells which are essential to the body's defence against infection. If this starts to happen, illness and even death can result.

This does not happen immediately the person is infected, however. The virus commonly lies dormant in the blood for a great many years, and it is thought that some individuals may have the virus and never develop any illness, though a great many do. Forecasts change from day to day, but current feeling is that much can be done to control the virus in its early stages, even keeping AIDS permanently at bay.

How is the virus transmitted?

By far the greatest number of people with the virus have acquired it through sexual contact. The virus is present in semen and vaginal fluid, and sexual acts that do not involve penetration hold little or no risk. Basically, it is possible to protect oneself and others by avoiding contact with or the sharing of body fluids such as vaginal fluid, blood and semen. The use of condoms during sexual activity, where semen, vaginal fluid or blood is present, is the safest way of reducing the risk of infection by the HIV virus.

The virus can also be transmitted by drug use, as mentioned earlier. The sharing of needles and syringes ('works') is extremely dangerous.

The virus is *not* transmitted through ordinary everyday contact such as kissing and hugging, or by the use of crockery, cutlery, towels or even a toilet that has been touched or used by a person carrying the virus

HIV/AIDS does not result from bi- or homosexuality but it does pose a risk for all sexually active people. AIDS will not be a problem for mutually faithful lifelong partners of any sexual orientation, but anal intercourse does pose additional transmission risks.

What about testing?

A test is now widely available through STD (sexually transmitted disease) or GU (genito-urinary) clinics and GPs. It is called the HIV Antibody Test (or sometimes, wrongly, the 'AIDS Test'), and looks for the presence of chemicals called antibodies which the human body produces in reaction to the presence of the virus.

Before going ahead with the HIV Antibody Test it is suggested that people ensure that *both* pre- and post-test counselling are offered. Some GPs are unable to provide adequate counselling or testing services and cannot offer a confidential service either. *Testing at GU clinics is covered by statutory regulations concerning confidentiality.* Take care to check on the above before deciding where to have an HIV Antibody Test.

What if the test is positive?

This means that the person has been infected with the virus at some time in the past and the body has produced antibodies against it. With many infections, antibodies are effective in ridding the infectious agent from the body, but against HIV they are ineffective. Once a person has been exposed to the virus – i.e., contracted it – they can pass it on to others. The use of condoms during sexual activity is therefore a vital necessity.

A *negative* result after the HIV Antibody Test means that the person has *probably* not been infected, but since the body can take up to three months to produce antibodies, there may be some question. A repeat test at a later date is usually recommended. *It does not mean that the person has AIDS.*

At Parents' Friend, we are still coming across parents who insist on an HIV/Antibody Test when they find out their son is gay. One mother, an ex-nurse, told her son to go for a test, and from then on the family refused to share his towel or use the same crockery. The woman then wondered why her son would not visit her. Her son was very upset by her attitude and unwillingness to read up on the subject and listen to others who actually knew more than she did about HIV/AIDS in spite of her nurse's training.

It is not the label given to people that makes them carriers of disease, it is whom they have sex with, how they have sex, how safely they have both had sex previously and also how safely they are practising sex now. Sex has as many descriptions and forms as there are sexually active people, male and female. Intelligence is necessary for *everyone*'s good health.

Some parents contact us when a son has been diagnosed HIV positive, and we support those parents from then on, for as long as necessary. Up to this point, no parent with a lesbian daughter or bisexual son has contacted us for support after finding their child is HIV positive.

The following contributions are from parents who have had to cope with HIV, AIDS, and even death.

Our son is very well at the moment, except that now he finds he can't live it up as much as he once did and has to take care of himself in sensible ways. He says he does not think he could possibly do a stressful job now, but has finished his college course with 'Outstanding Excellence', and his tutors have advised him to write. He has had a couple of articles printed, including one about the AZT discussion (having come off it a couple of years ago and finding himself much better without it). He is doing a lot of counselling and is in the process of setting up a support group in connection with one of the London AIDS support networks. His life is interesting and pleasant, even though the thought of AIDS must be faced and I feel that he has developed a pretty good philosophy about facing it. Our son still misses his lover dreadfully, but it doesn't seem to interfere with his positive attitude.

Having a son with the HIV virus seems to make little difference to us as his parents and as long as he remains as positive and busy as he is now, and is so obviously happy in himself, then we're happy too. Any problems in the future we will deal with as and when. . . .

Joan

*

I have a gay son, Peter, and a married daughter. Peter told me he was gay nine years ago, but he had known since he was thirteen. He is now twenty-eight.

Peter's partner, Simon, with whom he has lived for eight years, is a transsexual, but felt himself to be gay at the time when he and Peter got together. Later, Simon, being sure, as all transsexuals are, that he was 'born in the wrong body', had all the treatment to ensure he can live as a woman. However, when it came to the final operation, Simon was found to be HIV positive and the surgeon they approached said it was far too risky for Simon, because of the way such an operation could affect his immune system.

Peter now works and Simon (who is now known as Sue and who lives and dresses as a woman) is on invalidity benefit. They have now bought their own house so that's an achievement when they have had so much to deal with.

I pray to God that when Peter needs me to be strong for him, as he surely will, I'll be there. He did have an HIV test, which was negative, thankfully, but, as I've told him, I've coped with everything else – sickness, unemployment, senile dementia in two of my relations – what's one more thing? We'll take it as it comes. As a parting shot, I'll never be a grandma – not because my son is gay – but because my daughter has chosen not to have children.

Bernadette

*

*On my kitchen wall I have a photograph of a young man sitting
with his little dog by a stream in the sunshine. He is bright-eyed,
alert, smiling and very much alive. I have a newspaper cutting of
this same young man, two years later, sitting gaunt, haggard
and disfigured by cancer, in an AIDS ward in St Mary's Hospital, London. He is sharing a joke with the young woman sitting beside him with her hand on his scarred knee. He is my gay
'son-in-law' and she is Princess Diana.*

*Paul died of AIDS three and a half years ago and I shall never
forget him. He hurtled through life, reckless, extravagant, full of
zest for living and exceedingly brave. He fought death until the
last hour. Five days before his death he had persuaded my son to
take him to Paris, knowing he had very little time left and the
two of them celebrated – at Paul's wish – by having a slap-up
dinner at one of the best restaurants they could find.*

*When sent for, we rushed down to London, expecting to find
him in bed, but he was sitting waiting for us, a gin and tonic in
his hand – though by this time he barely had strength to speak.
He went to bed without help and he didn't see another day.*

*His funeral was an extraordinary affair. The big London church
was packed with all sorts and conditions of men and women and
I remember thinking, 'My self-righteous mother would have shown
most of them the door.' But love was there in abundance, even if
conformity was not.*

*Paul was carried out of church with Louis Armstrong's cracked
voice singing 'What a Wonderful World' and we wept tears which
turned to laughter as we left the church – for there, on the roof of
the leading hearse, was the dog Peanuts – life-size and made of
flowers. As we drove to the cemetery her tail wagged in the breeze
and people on the pavements smiled and waved as we passed.*

*Later, we all crowded into the flat and, as one does at funeral
parties, laughed, made light conversation and put off the coming
hour of reality. There was barely room to shut the front door and
I saw two people sitting in the bath, having an animated discussion. When most had drifted away, we went, with our son and a
few close friends, to the pub across the road – a noisy, garish
place – and laughed, sometimes cried, carrying on with the strange-
ness of the early hours of mourning. At least we had done what*

Paul wanted us to do: 'have a damn good party'.

Back at home our son lit a candle and set it in the window and I was overcome with intolerable desolation. We had left him behind and he would be cold and lonely, and then I remembered what Paul had once said: 'I'd like to be buried under a tree and then I can still be part of the earth.'

Joan

*

Steven never told me he had AIDS and I never asked – it just happened that I knew. He was the first-born of my seven children, five sons and two daughters and, as it happens with firstborns the world over, there was an extra bond between us. We were both Leos, so the love of beauty, the arts and show business in all its forms, was inherent in both our personalities. Steven was very gifted. He could make any old thing into a thing of beauty. As a very small child he amazed us all with the lovely things he would create out of bits and pieces that other people would throw away. This gift he carried with him right to the end of his short life.

It was only a matter of time before Steven moved to London where he worked in the theatre and then on to Los Angeles where he lived for twelve years. Los Angeles was to become his home and his final resting place.

Steven and I rang each other nearly every week, always laughing and joking and catching up on gossip. I was happy when he decided to share a house with his friend Susan. Not because I thought that maybe the two of them might have some sort of romantic involvement but, thinking back, I felt that he would not be alone and he would have a friend to turn to in his bad times. I always prayed that if my children could have one gift it would be that they had someone to love who would love them in return.

I was aware, from the time Steven was a very young teenager, that he was gay. To me it was all a part of him being the person he was (and as one of his brothers said, when he found out Steven had AIDS, 'If anyone can beat it he will – he's special'). I won't say I didn't worry about his homosexuality because I did, knowing how prejudiced people could be against gay people. All I could give was my love and support and I thank God for that. If I had been any other way I wouldn't be able to live with myself today.

Steven must have known for a long time that he was HIV positive. He had been a manic depressive since childhood and, when he retreated into himself, his brothers (who followed him to L.A. and lived in the same apartment block) thought it was one of his depressive periods. But as he began to lose weight and look ill, they began to worry about him. That was about the time he decided to give up his apartment and move in with Susan.

After that period he looked a picture of health. Susan was, no doubt, feeding him up, helping him financially (as he wasn't working at that time) and I found out later he was taking lots of vitamins and it appeared to be doing him a lot of good. He was always a good-looking boy and at that time he looked tanned and healthy. Seeing him, no one would have guessed how ill he was.

I remember about a year later I phoned him and he was about to go to see a doctor as he didn't feel well. He had resumed work and had been working for some time. As it was, he was feeling very ill and trying very hard to keep his job, but, so as not to worry me, he made light of his doctor's visit. From that time on things began to go wrong. It was July 4th – Independence Day – when Steven went into hospital, and so began months of the most painful medical tests. All the time Susan was at his side, working all day and spending every minute she could with him. As always, when he was in any trouble, he kept it all from me so I wouldn't worry and never once was the word AIDS mentioned or implied. As time went on I became more and more worried and decided to go and see Steven and Susan. When I arrived I began to realize how bad things were and just how ill he was. He tried for two days to put on a brave face, hoping that he wouldn't have to return to hospital before I left, but it wasn't to be; his lungs were very bad by this time as he had contracted pneumocystis and he coughed constantly day and night. On the Thursday morning he was so ill his doctor wanted him back in hospital but he begged to be allowed to stay at home until I went back to England. That evening, although he was very ill, the two of us walked in the sunshine to the French Market Place to eat. We walked along that evening and I looked at his thin face, still beautiful in spite of all his suffering, and he said 'You know, Mum, I wish I'd come back home five years ago when things were good, but then

I stayed too long at the fair.' I can remember having to fight back the tears as he seemed so young and helpless and I knew I was helpless to do anything about it.

Steven lived a further six months – six months of unbelievable pain and agony. I thank God I was with him when he died but our walk together that spring evening was the last time we walked in the sunshine together. The week before he died he would plan every day to go for that walk but it was always tomorrow and I knew it would never happen.

Steven's death was the worst thing that ever happened to me in my life, but it's amazing how, with time, a calmness seems to take over from the terrible heartbreak. I will never get over losing my beloved son but we were able to say the things that were in our hearts, in his last week.

We were able to talk and laugh about the times we'd shared, both good and bad. I like to think he was ready to leave us when the time came, as he had said his goodbyes to us all as he slipped away. His last words to me were 'Mum, let me go.'

Valerie

*

My son died over two years ago but I am haunted by the memory of our dreadful ordeal. We lived a life of total secrecy and lies and built a wall of fear around ourselves. He had many friends and it is only recently that I asked one of them if they knew about his homosexuality and that he died with AIDS. His friend was so shocked and sad that my son had been unable to tell anyone. He only ever told me and I was totally unable to cope with it at the time. But despite my efforts to get help there did not seem to be anyone around to talk to.

I am grateful now that our love kept us together and, indeed, grew stronger as his illness progressed but I was never able to meet another parent and was shocked on my many vigils in hospital in London to find so many people dying alone. We met a priest who helped us both to come to terms with our situation and we both converted to Catholicism. At least my son had a beautiful funeral. The priest still visits me and helped me to bury my son's ashes in June of this year.

*I wish to share a scribble I found among my son's papers re-
cently. I don't know when he wrote it but I never knew he felt so
alone. He always seemed so cheerful and was obviously suffering
terribly.*

*I imagined once that God inhabited
Silence – serene, calm, beneficent.
So I told the doctor 'Don't worry I'll be alright. Set up the
drip, close the door.'*

*He wanted to send me to sleep, said he,
But I wasn't having that – not me.*

*'Leave me alone,' said I, calmly, 'to contemplate some poetry.'
He closed the door.
I picked up my book and waited. . . .
I have never felt so utterly alone.
The words in my book would not be read.
My eyes pierced the pages, but the only things I could actually
see were bare, white, spaces.*

*I have never felt to utterly alone.
My body would not matter any more.
I bit my thumb to feel the pain.
To get back down to my book again –
But nothing mattered.*

*I succumbed to the stifling silence and stillness.
They took me away – away.
My movements, my mind, my being, was theirs
And they showed me myself for what I was.*

*I have never felt so utterly alone.
Reading? Why? What is there to learn?
I ought to want to live again –
To feel, to breathe, experience –
But – to have more, and more, and more – of the same –
Would that make any difference?*

                                                                    Kay

*

Much has been written about the devastation of AIDS and its effect on the family. What hope is there for those of us who feel we are in limbo, knowing that a loved one has tested positive for the HIV virus, not knowing if and when symptoms will develop that bring a diagnosis of AIDS? How do we cope with this knowledge, with the fear and the uncertainty?

It's been five years (on Halloween) since my son told me his test results. I had to ask him – he had not wanted to tell me. In fact, he had not wanted to take the test at all, until his work on the hotline at the Gay Community Center prompted him to do so. Steve was 28 then, in 1986, and I had known that he is gay since he shared with me at the age of 19. I was concerned about the test results, of course, but not having a great deal of information other than that AIDS attacks the immune system, the only thing I knew to do was to hug him and then deliver motherly advice on how he could keep his immune system healthy by eating right, losing weight, getting enough sleep, exercising and giving up smoking and drinking. This was not well received.

I realized I couldn't live his life for him, even though I gladly would have, but I could do something. I could learn about HIV/ AIDS, and maybe I could help others along the way. I wanted to know what to expect, what might happen. I took 'buddy' training at the local AIDS Services Foundation, which included information on medical, psychological and emotional issues, and then was assigned to my first PWA (person with AIDS) – a woman, my age, with three grown sons and a background very similar to mine. I was Sharon's buddy for ten months until she died the day after Christmas, four years ago. I believe she did far more for me than I was able to do for her. She taught me the value of a positive attitude, of 'going for the flow' because each day was different and we never knew what to expect. Most of all she taught me the absolute need for hope. Her wonderful sense of humor kept us both going at the toughest times. I will always be grateful for the experience of Sharon, even though she broke my heart at the time.

That same year, at the Parents FLAG Convention in Washington D.C., I was motivated to become part of a task force formed

to respond to the needs of families touched by AIDS. The Family
AIDS Support Project was created, to distribute educational materials and establish a nationwide support network.

My son indicated his appreciation for my involvement, but
remained uncommunicative about his own needs. It was important for me to tell him how much I care, to ask him to please not
shut me out, and to tell him that I wanted to walk this walk with
him. Then we set about making plans for a trip to England together, where I was born and raised and where he had always
wanted to explore his roots. We managed to pull that off within
a year, and it was the happiest of times. a memory that will live
with me forever.

It wasn't until Steve's 32nd birthday in January 1990, that I
experienced the depths of despair. I knew that he had been for a
physical check-up because he had been feeling fatigued, that a
blood test showed that his immune system was depressed (below
500 T-cells) and that he was awaiting results from a second blood
test a month after the first one. It was at his birthday dinner that
he told me that the doctor had started him on AZT that day.
After he left, I cried myself to sleep, slept fitfully for an hour or
so, then woke up crying and couldn't stop. I have never felt so
alone in my entire life. I cried for two days, absolutely devastated
emotionally. I was shocked by my reaction, since I had thought I
was prepared for this, after being involved for so many years. I
discovered that it's not possible to be prepared.

However, through it all, I knew intellectually that I was going
through a grieving process – the denial, the anger, the overwhelming
feeling of hopelessness. I had to accept the reality that my son
might get sick and even die, experience the pain of knowing that,
re-establish hope, and figure out how to adjust to going on living.

The first thing I discovered was that I was not alone, that all
I had to do was to reach out. One telephone call to another mother
of a gay son sent out waves that brought me more caring and
concern than I had ever experienced in any situation. No one had
realized how vulnerable I was, including me! I was always in
control, taking charge, helping others. And helping others was
still the answer for me. As a result of letting it be known how
devastated and vulnerable I was, making people aware that I was
obviously not the only parent who felt this way, I was allowed to

start a support group for people with concerns about HIV at our monthly Parents FLAG meetings, something I had been wanting to do for some time, and which the chapter had not felt was needed. It reinforced my belief that everything happens for a reason, and something good comes out of everything.

Steve remains asymptomatic and has developed a positive outlook and a healthier lifestyle. He became involved in a support group, and told me that, in his group of six gay men, he was the only one who could be open and receive emotional support from his family. This demonstrates the overwhelming need for us to be supportive of our children.

My new hope is that the AZT will keep Steve healthy until a cure is found; for strength, better communication and healing within my own family and the best quality of life for my son.

Please know, as I do, that whatever comes, you will do your best, and you will survive. Learn to put the 'downers' on the back burner and live with hope. And always remember: you are not alone.

Pat

Conclusion

Instead of seeing the rug being pulled from under us, we can learn to dance on the shifting carpet.

Thomas Crum

I chose to conclude this anthology with a selection of pieces from parents who are still struggling and others who have transformed ignorance into understanding and acceptance.

I have three children, a son and two daughters. My youngest daughter was still living at home. She has always been so very feminine, enjoying all the girlie things – dolls, pretty dresses, hair ribbons. As a teenager she had boyfriends and went through all the phases of 'being in love' with this boy and that boy or thinking this pop star or that was fab!

When she was about 16 she started going out at weekends, drinking and night-clubbing with friends. We were worried sick. One particular male friend, unknown to us, was gay, and Angie went with him often to gay clubs. (We found this was a gay club only later.) She then became friends with a group of girls at this club, but we never met them. About ten months ago she brought a girl home and I've done my best to welcome her. Things began to get very strained between us, neither admitting what we both knew.

I realized that if I didn't want to drive her away for the wrong reasons I would have to ease off and let her live her own life.

We have done everything we can to assure Angie we love her and will always be here. What I can't tell her is it's tearing me apart. Members of our extended family are asking awkward questions, which I'm not handling very well. I'm also withdrawing from my own friends in case they find out.

Angie is also afraid of people finding out; in some ways she's ashamed of her relationship and won't introduce her friend to anyone.

We still love our daughter but feel we'll need a lot of support for a long, long time.

Mary

*

This morning seemed like any other until I picked up that letter hiding among the bills.

My daughter, Ann, had joined the Army a few months previously and I had not seen her for at least three months. I decided to open Ann's letter first but as I began to read the first few lines the excitement I felt earlier began to subside, to be replaced by a sickening feeling in my stomach. It began

Dear Mum,

This letter may come as a shock but I thought you might like to know that I will be bringing my friend home to meet you this weekend.

I recently fell in love with another female. I have found out that I'm bisexual.

The letter went on to tell me that she hoped I'd be able to understand and accept her and her friend. She also told me that if I had any difficulty accepting them — and she realized there might be a problem — then she would respect my wishes and not bring her friend home to meet me. The letter ended with:

I love you Mum.

Ann

I found myself getting up in a kind of daze, unable to take in all the implications. Why did I not recognize what she must have been feeling every time I asked her why she didn't go out with her girl friends to a dance? She had always replied, 'Don't worry about me, Mum. I'm happy enough at home with my drawing and painting and listening to my music. Besides, my friends are all hanging around street corners with young lads.'

Although the news had come as a shock, I had to ask myself why she did not confide in me sooner. Did she think I would stop loving her because she wanted to lead an unconventional lifestyle as opposed to what we call conventional?

I decided to telephone Ann and I don't know how I managed to stop myself crying over the telephone but I found myself saying that I had received her letter and I was pleased she would be bringing her friend home for the weekend. I learned that her friend was a sergeant, 32 years old, who had been in the Army for twelve years.

I survived the weekend but what I would have given to have someone with whom I could discuss this, as I knew in no way could I speak about it with my ex-husband without my daughter's permission. Also I hadn't spoken to her father for over a year, so it didn't seem the right thing to do anyway.

My son was staying with his father at the time and I didn't wish to discuss it with him either until I knew what my daughter wanted. My own family live in Dublin and I live in England. As we are from a strong Catholic background, I felt it would not have been appropriate to mention it.

Not long after my daughter's visit I decided to go over to Dublin to visit my mother. Whilst there I decided to visit my father's grave. At the cemetery I noticed that the two graves next to my father's were those of two young men, 17 and 18 years of age. Their photographs had been placed into the headstones with the explanation of how they had been killed on a motor-cycle whilst travelling home to see their parents.

I stood transfixed, thinking of what the parents of these boys must have felt when they heard this sad and devastating news. How, long ago, perhaps these same parents had been thinking of what kind of life they would like their sons to live. Had they hoped they would be doctors, solicitors, artists, poets, fathers and husbands, rich and famous or just happy in their chosen lifestyle? I thought of how I would feel if that was my daughter lying there, 'cut down' before she knew what it was like to be 'in love', to enjoy the things she was doing now – skiing, paragliding, absailing, sailing, driving, going out with her friends bowling, swimming and enjoying life. Those mothers would never see their sons again in this life. I have my daughter. *I love her, she loves me and I will see her as often as she has the time to come and visit me. So what if she has chosen to lead her life in this unconventional way; at least she's alive and happy and I will always stand beside her and support her.*

Mina

One mother suspected that her son might be gay, but this did not prevent the shock when she knew for sure. That knowledge also provided her with new insight on human sexuality:

When my son was about nine years old I was concerned about him. Somehow he was different from any other children I knew and I was very afraid that he might be gay. To this day I do not know what it was that made me suspect this but I had a very real fear about it.

As with most of the people I know, I had been brought up very ignorant about non-heterosexual people. Although I had known that a couple of my parents' friends were gay, this was never spoken of – they were acceptable because they didn't make an issue of it. The only information that I had been given was that homosexuality was disgusting and a 'sin'. But my young son was not disgusting or sinful.

I had to find out more information and so I searched libraries and bookshops for some enlightened knowledge, so that if my fears were justified at least I would understand and be better able to cope. Much of what I read made me more worried than ever – the injustices that gay people face, the violence and prejudice really frightened me, but other things made me almost envious – fancy having a partner who really understood what period pains feel like!!

The more I read the more I realized that I had known nothing; every stereotypical character I had watched on telly, every joke I had laughed at, every vague idea of what they did in bed was based on an ignorant attitude passed on to me by a homophobic society. The thing that upset me most was reading about a young man killing himself rather than tell his parents he was gay. The prospect of this happening with my son frightened me far more than the idea of him being gay.

Although I didn't confide my fears to my husband, I did discuss a lot of what I had been reading (he thought I was very strange reading such stuff), and he too realized that he didn't really agree with the homophobic attitude he had been brought up with.

When my son was 14 he told me he thought he might be gay. Outwardly I was very calm. I assured him that it made no difference to me, I would always love him whatever he was and that I would always be there for him to talk to, but I also told him that

*he was very young to know for sure and warned him to be care-
ful whom he said anything to; once he told people he was gay it
would be very hard to tell them otherwise if this was 'just a
phase'. Inside I was in turmoil – all my worst fears were being
realized. My son was to become an outcast, he would lead a lonely
and loveless life, but at least he had told me.*

*It was quite some time before we spoke about it again. I began
to feel that perhaps I had been wrong in my worries and that
maybe it had been just a phase. However I had kept on reading
books and had learned a lot about sexuality in general. I had always
been very inhibited myself and had never been interested in sex.*

*I began to question my own sexuality quite seriously. I
met with a group of lesbians at the local women's centre,
partly because I had finally found some people that I could talk to
about my son, and partly out of curiosity about them and how I
would feel about them. I wasn't surprised that I didn't fancy any
of them. I didn't fancy any men either. I decided I was just an 'it'.*

*My son, on the other hand, was growing up. At 17 he told me
he was sure he was gay. After all the preparation I had had it
was still a bombshell. My new, huge fear was what his father
would say. Also, where would he meet other gay teenagers? By
this time I had made friends with several gay men and women
where I worked and they were very helpful and supportive. My
husband had also got used to the company of my gay friends and
I'm sure this all helped him when our son finally came out to
him. He told me later that all those discussions we had had in
the past, about what I had read, had made all the difference.*

*About this time my eldest son's live-in girlfriend left him for
another woman. I was afraid that this would make his acceptance
of his brother a lot harder, but it actually seemed to help him to
understand better and he was going to need that understanding
a lot more than we realized.*

*Was it really three years ago! I went to work, as usual, to the
counselling service where I was the receptionist. A young woman
called in to see if she could do any voluntary work for us. I took
to her instantly and quite looked forward to working with her.
There was something different about her, but it was some time
before I realized that she was gay. She and my son got on well. I
clearly remember them giggling about the 'just a phase' attitude
they had received from people.*

I know that I felt from the start that she was special, but I gradually realized that I was falling in love with her. Not the friendly, sisterly kind of love that I felt for my closest friends but an emotional and physical attraction like I had never felt before. Here I was, 40 years old, married for twenty-three years and only now beginning to understand my own sexuality! The most amazing thing was finding that she felt the same about me.

But what were we to do about it? What about my family? We couldn't avoid hurting other people if we were to have any happiness of our own, but had I the right to be so selfish? People were still coming to terms with my son being gay, how could I tell them I was too?

It seems incredible but my husband was the most supportive person that I told. He was genuinely happy for me and helped me to tell our sons and my mother. Even now, when I get choked up with guilt, he tells me that I deserve this happiness, that I gave them everything for twenty-three years and now I have my reward. He didn't want the family to break up and would have preferred my partner to move in with us than for me to move out, but this would have been too difficult for everyone. So instead he helped me to move, and is always at the other end of the phone if we need each other. Most important to me is that he has promised not to try and claim custody of our other son who lives with my partner and me.

I hate the hurt I have caused my family and only hope that they do understand how important it is to me to be myself, to be complete. Maybe this is just a phase I am going through and one day I will feel differently. But I will never regret this phase. I have a relationship that is worth everything that society throws at us. If we cannot be out to some of our associates, that is their loss. And I really do understand how my partner feels when she has period cramps!

Katrina

*

For some time I'd thought Kieron could be gay but never asked him, mainly because I didn't want to hear the answer. I knew that in time he would tell me, if indeed that was the case.

Kieron finally told me that he was gay. I thought I had prepared myself for it but it hit me like a ton of bricks. I was numb, and to be honest I was a walking liability. I couldn't eat, sleep or anything. I just kept hitting the bottle to block it all out. I just couldn't cope.

The thought of sex repulsed me – any sort of sex. Gay sex haunted me each time I shut my eyes. I saw the sordid side of S.M., bondage, condoms, AIDS, anal sex – not forgetting blow jobs! I was really at the bottom and couldn't seem to bring my-self up at all.

A few days before Christmas I looked at Kieron and thought, I knew you were gay before you told me – you haven't changed, I have! I gave him a cuddle and told him I still loved him more than life and I was ready to learn if he was ready to show me that it's not all bad. If he could go at my speed I was sure I could learn. If he didn't rush things and we could work this out together, I'd make it. I told him he'd had a long time to accept all this but I was only just beginning. Would he be here for me to answer all my questions and never lie to me? Kieron just hugged me tight, saying, 'Take as long as you like Mum, we'll get there together in the end. Time isn't important.'

We went over all my fears, of AIDS, etc., and he told me all about safer sex. I can honestly say I would have never come so far without him. His patience was never-ending. It didn't matter to him how many times I asked a question, he would go over and over it until I understood. He explained how his going out with girls had been his way of trying to be the 'norm', or what society expects. He had really tried but it didn't work. Then he explained that, yes, he could get married, have kids, but why? He knew that he would always be pulled back to being gay and if he was discovered it would mean he was hurting a wife, kids, in-laws, grandparents. Why cause all that pain to so many? I couldn't fault him. Of course he was right.

We agreed to keep it secret at first, until I felt strong enough to cope with comments from outside. Then Kieron said he was bringing two of his friends home. I was shell-shocked! All I could think was of me having two poofs in my home – not really think-ing that my own son was one too. Yet, after half an hour I was surprised just how comfortable they were, talking about gay issues. Kieron took them home and I went to bed thinking I'd made a real hash of it. When Kieron came back, he told me how his friends had thought I was brilliant and how they were going to come back to see me.

In the new year I tried to be more positive but did slide into depressions at times.

Kieron's dad now knew and wasn't too pleased. Each time Kieron went through the door, his dad would go on about 'The best gay is a dead gay', and I tried to help him to understand. He'd say 'They should all be shot' or 'They should all be put in a camp to live together'. In fact, if we'd had a gun I'm sure he'd have used it on Kieron, he felt so bad about him. So, while trying my very best, Kieron and I were having daily grief from his dad. I knew I had to decide whether to go along with Kieron's dad for a quiet life or take the rough ride with Kieron. All I heard from his dad was the negative side, but at the same time, the positive side from Kieron. I simply couldn't reject my son or kick him out.

At work I had it pretty tough. Nobody knew about Kieron and that was how I wanted it to stay. I put up with all the things people said about the gays at work.

Soon afterwards I told an in-law who worked with me and I didn't beat about the bush. She told Kieron it made no difference, nothing would ever change between him and herself, and she did me the great favour of telling her side of the family. I told my own side, and waited for their reaction, expecting rows and rejection. One uncle I'd thought would be the most difficult turned up trumps; another uncle we'd thought would be fine doesn't speak to us now. You win some, you lose some!

I found telling my family really hard, but I'd made it clear to all of them that should they reject Kieron, they were rejecting me. They accepted it – every one of them. On my down days I'm now able to ring someone.

I feel sorry for any parent who is just finding out they have a gay child, because I know what the next few months could hold for them. I would, however, advise them to try to keep an open mind once they are over the shock.

Dinah

Pat, from California, helps to make the point that it is the same wherever you might live:

Hi! My name is Pat Paddock. I live in California, am the mother of four children, and my 35-year-old son happens to be gay. He shared this with me 17 years ago last February 11th at 5.35 p.m. It was the last news I wanted to hear.

I was very naïve and uninformed at the time. I didn't know anything about homosexuality except the nasty rumors I'd heard. During my son's high school years, when he was so lonely and moody, I had suspected that he might be gay, but whenever that nagging suspicion popped up in the back of my mind I'd push it away, because it was too awful to think about. I hoped it would never be true, so I wouldn't have to deal with it.

When it did turn out to be true, the only thing that seemed important was to let my son know that I loved him and nothing he could ever tell me would change that. My reaction was, Hey, this is my son we're talking about now, and I know he's not any of those awful things I've heard. He's the same person I've always known and loved. He hasn't changed, so it has to be that my information is wrong, and it's up to me to educate myself. My only negative feeling was an overwhelming fear for his happiness and well being.

I got a lot of help from taking a human sexuality class at the time. I have a smart son: I'd been in the class exactly one week when he told me that he's gay. He knew I was in a good place to get some help!

The two things I learned that helped me the most were, first of all: gay people don't choose to be gay. Even the experts can't agree on what causes our sexuality, but they do at least agree that it's determined at a very early age, and the latest studies indicate that it's probably predetermined.

And secondly, I learned how many gay people there are. I thought my son was the first gay person I'd ever known, and I was afraid he was going to lead a very lonely life. I learned that at least one in every ten people is gay, and one in every three or four families has a gay member.

I believe that sexual orientation has nothing to do with a person's worth as a human being. It's only one part of a total person – a very important part.

I am proud that my son chose to share this part of his life with me, and grateful for the trust he placed in me not to reject him,

*because I know now that coming out to parents is the most diffi-
cult thing a gay person chooses to do – taking a risk of suffering
the ultimate rejection by the people who created his/her very being. The wall my son built up between us came tumbling down,
the wall that said, 'Don't get too close, because if you know who
I really am, you won't love me any more'.*

*For a whole year, I didn't know another parent of a gay child.
Then I heard about Parents and Friends (now Parents, Families
and Friends) of Lesbians and Gays, USA, a support group for
parents of gay children, to help them understand and accept their
gay children and for gay people dealing with family-related issues.
Believing very strongly in peer support, and wanting to meet
other parents, I started a local chapter 'behind the Orange Cur-
tain' in conservative Orange County, California.*

*My personal recommendation for parents is first of all to meet
other parents, so you really know you're not alone; then, meet and
talk with gay people and really listen to their stories of what life
has been like for them; and educate yourself to learn the truth and
dispel the myths and stereotypes. Above all, give your child unconditional love and acceptance. S/he hasn't changed – it's your expectations of what life was going to be like for this child that have to
change. Give yourself time to grieve for the loss of those expectations,
then work on establishing expectations based on truth and reality.*

*

*It had been difficult for Rachel to admit to herself that she was
'lesbian', a word she had been conditioned to associate with 'abnormal' and 'not nice'. I felt a great sense of relief that the secret
was at last out in the open. My next concern was to understand
and accept that Rachel was non-heterosexual. A much more difficult task was to get other members of the family to come to terms
with it! At one point I feared that my husband and my elder
daughter, Joanne, might reject Rachel. Joanne had described Rachel
as 'bent' and 'queer' and stated that she would never be prepared
to accept that her sister was a lesbian.*

*Four months later, Rachel was involved in a horrific car acci-
dent and sustained many injuries, not least of which was a broken
neck. During the many hours spent at Rachel's bedside, frantic
with worry as to whether she would recover and have full use of her*

limbs, it suddenly occurred to me that we had never once, during this time, discussed Rachel's sexuality. The accident and the worry about whether she would pull through had put everything into its proper perspective. My ex-husband, Mike, and I both agreed we would prefer a happy, healthy, alive lesbian to a dead daughter.

It is life itself that is important and not just one small facet of a person's make-up that is slightly different from what society defines as 'normal'.

Three years on from Rachel's coming out, I now feel honoured and privileged to have been given the opportunity to meet and to get to know many of Rachel's friends. As a result of this experience, I feel that I have grown into a much stronger and more enlightened person. I can say with the most heartfelt sincerity that Rachel and her friends have enriched my life; they have added a whole new dimension and have brought me an enormous amount of pleasure.

Barbara

*

I have, through my son's being gay, set my stall out to learn about sexual orientation and to meet people of all sexualities and have wonderful gay friends.

I think the worst thing you can do to anyone is to put a label on them. I'm sure that prevents them from growing. I prefer to regard people as whole and complete – body, mind, spirit – and to focus on their sexuality is diminishing. I am convinced that there is more to love than sexuality and that equality and loving responsibility are the final criteria for valuing any sexual relationship, whatever its origin and gender composition.

Amy

What emerges clearly from each piece included in this anthology is the way contributors felt a need to look afresh at their own lives and relationships with family and friends. This is something we rarely do without a crisis in our lives. There are a myriad of paths taken in an attempt to resolve the 'problem', as each contributor sees it, but each seems to reiterate the message of the first Parents' Friend handbook: 'It really is the heterosexuals in society who have the problem.'

Whatever your feelings, it is fine to have them, and it is just as acceptable to take the time you need to ponder.

Useful Contacts

KENRIC (social group for lesbian women)
write: BM Kenric, London, WC1N 3XX for regional info./nos.

L.I.S. (Lesbian Information Service)
01706–817235 or write: PO Box 8, Todmorden, OL14 5TZ

* LONDON BISEXUAL LINE
0181–569–7500
Tues. & Wed. 7.30 p.m. to 9.30 p.m.

* LONDON FRIEND (gay counselling)
0171–837–3337 (minicom)
Daily 7.30 p.m. to 10 p.m. (men & women)
0171–837–2782 (minicom)
Tues. & Thurs. 7.30 p.m. to 10 p.m. (women only)

* LONDON LESBIAN & GAY SWITCHBOARD
0171–837–7324 (24 hr.) please persevere

* LONDON LESBIAN LINE
0171–251–6911
Mon. & Fri. 2 p.m. to 10 p.m.
Tues. to Thurs. 7 p.m. to 10 p.m.

*Regional information can be obtained from these numbers

NATIONAL AIDS HELPLINE (24 hr.)
Freephone 0800–567123
Freephone 0800–521361 (minicom)
10 a.m. to 10 p.m.

For regional HIV/AIDS advice/info. see AIDS in telephone directory

PASTELS (Partners' & Spouses' Telephone Support)
Subsidiary of Parents' Friend
For heterosexuals who find they have a lesbian, gay or bisexual
partner

0113–267–4627 (Joy/Alan) or 0113–257–7523 (Valerie)
7.30 p.m. to 11 p.m. best, but you may try daytime
(answerphone on both nos.)

Should you wish to discuss any worry you have relating to your
faith and how it affects the way you feel about your lesbian, gay
or bisexual daughter or son, ring any of the following numbers:

GAY & LESBIAN HUMANIST ASSOCIATION
01926–58450
34 Spring Lane, Kenilworth,
Warks. CV8 2HB

JEWISH LESBIAN & GAY HELPLINE
0171–706–3123
Mon. & Thurs. 7 p.m. to 10 p.m.

LESBIAN & GAY CHRISTIAN MOVEMENT
0171–587–1235
Wed. & Sun. 7 p.m. to 10 p.m.
Oxford House, Derbyshire St.,
London E2 6HG

QUEST (for gay Catholics)
0171–792–0234
Fri./Sat./Sun. 7 p.m. to 10 p.m. or write:
BM Box 2585, London WC1X 3XX

RELIGIOUS SOCIETY OF FRIENDS (QUAKERS)
0171–387–3601
or write: Quaker Home Service,
Friends House, 173 Euston Road
London NW1 2BJ

Parent contact groups mentioned in this book:

LEEDS: PARENTS' FRIEND (Reg. Charity No. 1002640)
c/o Voluntary Action Leeds
Stringer House, 34 Lupton St.
Hunslet, LEEDS, LS10 2QW
0113–267–4627 (Joy/Alan)
0113–257–7523 (Valerie)
7.30 p.m. to 11 p.m. best (answerphone when unavailable at
other times)

LEICESTER: 0116–255–0667
7.30 p.m. to 10.30 p.m.

SHEERNESS (Kent): ACCEPTANCE
01796–661463
Tues. to Fri. 7 p.m. to 9 p.m.

You can check whether there is a parents' helpline in your own area by ringing one of the above three phone numbers.

If you feel comfortable with your lesbian, gay or bisexual daughter or son you may wish to be somewhat 'political'. You can wave your banner or campaign for lesbian and gay equality by contacting **FFLAG (Families & Friends of Lesbians and Gays)**, which was set up in 1993 for this purpose.
Write: PO Box 153, Manchester M60 1LP

In the USA

PARENTS FAMILIES AND FRIENDS OF LESBIANS AND GAYS (PFLAG)
1012 14th Street N.W., Suite 700, Washington, DC 20005
With chapters and contacts all over the USA, PFLAG is the best parents' resource available. PFLAG also has a task force on spouses of lesbians and gays and a task force on children who love someone gay.

NATIONAL GAY AND LESBIAN TASK FORCE INFORMATION LINE
(202) 332–6483

There are many gay and lesbian centres and information lines at the local level. See directory for details.

BISEXUAL INFORMATION & COUNSELING SERVICES
599 West End, New York, NY 10024

NATIONAL AIDS INFORMATION HOT LINE
1–800–342–AIDS

Reading List

The following books have proved helpful and interesting to parents over the years. Most if not all of these books can be ordered from the bookshops mentioned at the end of the list. All orders from these shops are sent under plain cover. Because prices change and postage costs have to be allowed for, we suggest confirming these details with individual shops before ordering.

AS WE ARE   By Don Clark. Published by Alyson Publications, USA. ISBN 1–55583–127–3. Offers sensitive, intelligent guidance to gay people and those who care about them.

BEING LESBIAN   By Lorraine Trenchard. Published by GMP Publishers. ISBN 0–85449–113–9. After reading it, one mother of a lesbian daughter remarked 'I didn't like it but I'm so glad I read it!' Don't read the bits you don't want to.

Bi ANY OTHER NAME   Edited by Loraine Hutchins and Lani Kaahumanu. Published by Alyson Publications, USA. ISBN 1–55583–174–5. Bisexual people speak out.

BISEXUAL LIVES   By bisexuals about themselves. Published by Off Pink Publishing. ISBN 0–9512103–0–5. Unfortunately this book is now out of print, but it may be available at your library.

COMING OUT TO PARENTS   By Mary V. Borhek. Published by Pilgrim Press, USA. ISBN 0–8298–0665–2. Valuable advice for lesbians, gay men and their parents.

DIFFERENT DAUGHTERS   Edited by L. Rafkin. Published by Cleis, USA. ISBN 0–939416–13–1. A collection of pieces written by mothers of lesbian daughters.

DIRT, GREED AND SEX   By L.W. Countryman. Published by SCM Press. ISBN 0–334–00327–X. A profound book on the sexual ethics in the New Testament and their present-day implications.

A GUIDE FOR PARENTS WHO HAVE LESBIAN, GAY OR BI-SEXUAL CHILDREN   By Joy Dickens. Available from Parents' Friend, c/o Voluntary Action Leeds, Stringer House, 34 Lupton Street, LEEDS LS10 2QW (£3.50 inc. p&p). A simple guide for parents and others wishing to understand homosexuality, with a foreword by Sir Ian McKellen.

HOW TO BE A HAPPY HOMOSEXUAL   By Terry Sanderson. Published by GMP Publishers. ISBN 0–948982–00–4. For gay men, but very useful and readable by anyone interested. Especially good on giving parents a better understanding of their gay sons. Again, don't read the parts you don't want to.

IS THE HOMOSEXUAL MY NEIGHBOR?   By Letha Scanzoni and Virginia Ramey Mollenkott. Published by Harper & Row. ISBN 0–06–067076–2. A Christian view by two outstanding evangelical authors, offering guidelines and inviting Christians to understand homosexuality without bias or preconceptions.

LESBIAN/WOMAN   By Del Martin and Phyllis Lyon. Published by Volcano Press, USA. ISBN 0–912078–91–X.

LIVING IN SIN   By Bishop John Spong of Newark, New Jersey, USA. Published by Harper & Row. ISBN 0–9514399–0–1. A wonderful book touching on all the untouchable or touchy subjects in the Bible and in the church itself, including homosexuality.

THE NEW LOVING SOMEONE GAY   By Don Clark. Published by Celestial Arts. ISBN 0–89087–505–7. A very helpful book for anyone who loves someone gay.

THE OTHER SIDE OF THE CLOSET   By Amity Pierce Buxton. Published by IBS Press, Inc. ISBN 1–877880–07–8. Written for those who find they have non-heterosexual partners. The best book of its kind.

PARENTS OF THE HOMOSEXUAL   By David K. Switzer and Shirley Switzer. Edited by Wayne E. Oates. Published by The Westminster Press, USA. ISBN 0–664–24327–4. Shows how, from a Christian perspective, a reconciliation between parents and homosexual children can be a real possibility.

PARENTS MATTER   By Ann Muller. Published by Naiad Press,

Inc., USA. ISBN 0–930044–91–6. Discusses parents' relationships with lesbian daughters and gay sons.

POSITIVELY WOMEN   Edited by Sue O'Sullivan and Kate Thompson. Published by Sheba Feminist Press. ISBN 0–90–717947–9. True stories of women and HIV/AIDS.

A STRANGER IN THE FAMILY   By Terry Sanderson. Published by Other Way Press. ISBN 0–948982–03–9. How to cope if your child is gay. Received mixed reviews.

TIME FOR CONSENT   By Norman Pittinger. Published by SCM Press. ISBN 0–334–01660–6. A Christian approach to homosexuality, and an open treatment of a subject that remains in the twilight of ethical concern.

Bookshops

There may well be an alternative/gay bookshop in your area and some of the major bookshops are now likely to have at least some of the above books in stock.

Gay's the Word
66 Marchmont Street, London WC1N 1AB (0171–278–7654).

Lesbian & Gay Christian Movement (LGCM) Bookshop
Oxford House, Derbyshire Street, Bethnal Green, London E2 6HG (0171–739–1249).

West & Wilde
24a Dundas Street, Edinburgh, Scotland EH3 6QQ (0131–556–0079).